An OT and SLP Team Approach

Sensory and Communication Strategies That WORK!

STUDENT SERVICES DEPARTMENT
SNOQUALMIE VALLEY SCHOOL DISTRICT
P.O. BOX 400
SNOQUALMIE, WA 98065-0400
425/831-8000

Nancy Kashman, BS, LOTR & Janet Mora, MA, CCC-SLP

Sensory RESOURCES
Las Vegas

© 2002 by Nancy Kashman and Janet Mora

All marketing and publishing rights guaranteed to and reserved by:

Sensory RESOURCES LLC
2200 E. Patrick Lane, Suite 3A
Las Vegas, NV 89119
(702) 433-0404
(888) 357-5867
Fax: (702) 891-8899
E-mail: info@sensoryresources.com
Internet: www.SensoryResources.com

All rights reserved. Printed in the United States of America. No part of this book may be produced in any manner without written permission of Sensory Resources LLC, except in the case of brief quotations embodied in reviews. Pages in the appendices of this book that include specific written permission may be reproduced in accordance with that permission. All trademarks used in this publication are the property of their respective owners.

It is the responsibility of the user of these materials to ensure that all activities are conducted with appropriate supervision. Exercise due care in selecting activities for a particular individual, especially with respect to safety, developmental level, and age-appropriateness. We recommend that you consult with trained professionals regarding interventions.

1st Edition, May, 2002

ISBN 1-931615-07-1

Dedication

This book is dedicated to our families without whose support we could never have completed our dream:

The Kashmans: Steve, Randi, Scott, Jennifer, Brian, Zachary Frank, Monia, and Frances Palaviccini

The Moras: Arthur, Jill, James, Alyson, Jim, and Barbara Glaser

A special thank you to The Chartwell Center; St. John The Baptist School System; Tammy Glaser, MS; Lorna Jean King, LOTR; Jennifer Kashman, LOTR; our editor, Polly McGlew; our publisher, David Brown; and all our special children and their families.

Table of Contents

Dedication 3

Introduction 9

Understanding Sensory Integration
   and Communication 11
   A Brief Look at Sensory Integration 11
   Communication and Sensory Integration 14

Sensory Processing Difficulties 21
   Vestibular System 21
   Proprioceptive System 25
   Tactile System 27
   Auditory System 31
   Visual System 34
   Olfactory System 35
   Oral/Feeding Difficulties 35

Sensory-Based Behaviors 39
   Sensory Defensiveness 39
   Self-Abusive and Self-Stimulating Behaviors 40
   Prompt Dependency 42
   Hierarchy of Prompts at a Glance 45

Approach to Intervention 47
   Therapeutic Approach at a Glance 49
   Treatment Cycle 50
   Teaming 51
   Benefits of Teaming 52

Assessment 55
    Communication 56
    Sensory Motor 58
    Environment 61
    Summary 62

The Environment 63
    Environmental Effects on Level of Arousal 63
    Environmental Strategies to Prepare for Learning 64
    Additional Environmental Strategies 72
    Environmental Visual Supports 77

Intervention 83
    Treatment Strategy Guidelines to Facilitate
        Learning and Communication 84
    Sensory and Communication-Based
        Treatment Strategies for Children 86
    Weighted and Pressure Touch Equipment 107
    Sensory and Communication-Based Treatment
        Strategies for the Adult and Older Child 110
    Vocational/Enterprise Activities 114
    Transitions and Waiting 115
    Informational Tools 118
    Oral and Feeding Treatment 121

Developing Communication Skills 127
    Individuals with Severe Difficulties 127
    Individuals with Moderate Difficulties 129
    Individuals with Mild Difficulties 130
    Using Visuals to Communicate 132

Using Videos 139
   Guidelines for the Production
      of Intervention Videos 142

Teaming Case Studies 145

Appendices 149

Sensory Integration Disorders 151
   The Autism Spectrum 151
   Disorders with Autistic Features 153
   Conditions With Sensory Integration Difficulties ... 155

Guide to Assessment of Environment 157

Stuffed Pants 161

Stuffed Sweatshirt 163

Weighted Vests 165

Oral Box 167

Example of a Fact Sheet 169
   Pamela's Strengths and Challenges 169
   Tips for Interacting with Pamela 170

General Communication Tips 173

References 175
   Assessment Sources 175
   Recommended Readings 176
   Organizations and Journals 181
   Resources 182
   E-mail 183

Introduction

Individuals diagnosed with autism, Asperger's Syndrome, PDD-NOS, and other challenges like as cerebral palsy, Down Syndrome, and attention deficit disorder, frequently exhibit not only communication difficulties but also a vast array of sensory integration issues. Any one or a combination of the senses can be affected: sight, hearing, touch, taste, smell, proprioception (sense of where one's body is in space), or vestibular (balance). Furthermore, the difficulty can be one of hyposensitivity or hypersensitivity.

Language and communication difficulties follow an equally diverse nature. Some children can hardly verbalize, whereas others possess highly developed expressive language but have impairments in their functional use of speech. Whatever the combination of language and sensory challenges, these difficulties can impact widespread areas of development, including social interactions, motor skills, academics, and self-esteem.

Traditionally, speech-language pathologists (SLPs) have addressed communication difficulties, and occupational therapists (OTs) have addressed sensory integration needs. In recent years, however, we have paid more attention to finding effective and functional solutions to the communication and sensory difficulties these children possess. Therapists have started working as a team for the benefit of the child with autism and sensory integration disorders. This has been especially true with speech-learning pathologists and occupational therapists.

Sensory integration techniques can modulate the level of arousal, thereby enhancing a person's ability to attend, function, and learn. When a child is engaged in more physical movement-related activities, therapists have found that he responds better to the efforts to elicit speech. A child often utters sounds, words, and sentences when bouncing, swinging, jumping, or running.

A team approach with individuals with autism spectrum disorder (ASD) and other developmental disorders involves not only the therapists, doctors, and other professionals, but also the parent/caregiver and (ideally) the individuals themselves. Teaming provides a holistic approach to facilitate skill development. Over time, teaming becomes trans-disciplinary as the interventionists assume each other's roles (when appropriate), and opportunities for learning become continuous.

We have developed the information and strategies presented in this book over a period of years. They provide a functional approach to working with children and adults with autism and sensory integration dysfunction. This book is a compilation of our own experiences, as well as suggestions and ideas shared by other professionals and parents. Within our practice and sharing our strategies with you, our goal is to enhance the developmental skills of individuals with sensory integration dysfunction, ASD, and other diagnoses, thereby providing them with an opportunity to participate more fully in functional life tasks and experience a more positive quality of life, both now and in the future.

Chapter One

Understanding Sensory Integration and Communication

A Brief Look at Sensory Integration

At an early age, children learn about themselves and the world around them by exploring, experiencing, and playing. With the use of their senses, and through their daily routines and interactions with others, children continuously gather, organize, and respond to information. Individuals who have sensory integration deficits may have difficulties in one or more areas of development, including communication, social interactions, academic learning, and recreational activities.

Sensory integration allows correct interpretation of experiences and appropriate responses to stimuli. It is the ability of the central nervous system to organize and process information from different sensory channels in order to produce an appropriate response.

An occupational therapist, Dr. Jean Ayres, developed the theory and treatment approach of sensory integration. This approach, which was initially used for children with learning difficulties, expanded over the years and is now used for individuals with many other diagnoses. Autism, cerebral palsy, Down Syndrome, developmental delays, Alzheimer's disease, and traumatic brain injury are only some of the disabilities that may exhibit sensory integration difficulties.

Sensory integration is the basis for all behavior. The central nervous system takes in information and enables the brain to register, filter out irrelevant information, integrate, organize, and respond appropriately. Accurate sensory processing allows for appropriate modulation or regulation of one's level of arousal and is the glue that basically "holds it all together." Sensory integration is an important foundation, influencing the acquisition of cognition, language, motor skills, self-help skills, and social and emotional well-being, which directly affect the quality of one's behaviors and skills.

There are seven senses. Vision, smell, touch, taste, and hearing are external sources of sensory input. The vestibular and proprioceptive systems are two, less-known, internal sensory sources that also provide necessary information. The vestibular system (sense of balance) and the proprioceptive system (body awareness) provide the feeling of movement and gravity.

Sensory integration evolves along a continuum, acquired through normal development, exploration, and play. Birth through ages seven to ten years is a particularly important time of sensory motor development and exploration. However, this skill continues to develop throughout life. Although changes may occur more rapidly in the child, the plasticity of the brain allows learning to be continuous. For the older child and adult, compensatory sensory strategies potentially enable them to participate more fully in life.

When sensory integration dysfunction occurs, the person cannot organize and integrate sensory input. The sensory experience is unpredictable, lacks meaning, and may affect a person quite differently from one time to another. This inconsistency places the individual in a high stress or anxiety mode—unprepared for learning new skills or participating in life tasks.

Breakdown in sensory integration may occur at various levels. Registration is the ability to perceive incoming information. This is our awareness meter, the first instant when we hear another's voice, smell cookies baking, or feel our hand against a cold tile. Difficulties occur when one is unable to adequately filter the incoming sensations and under- or over-registers sensory input. The individual who under-registers input receives less of it and may seek additional sensations or be unresponsive to sensory stimuli. Conversely, the individual who over-registers sensory input may present avoiding and defensive behaviors.

Integration and organization is the ability to take in information from a variety of sensory systems (multichannel input), make sense of it, and organize it for use. Difficulties can occur with single- or multichannel sensory input. Monochanneling refers to being only able to process one sensory channel at a time. For example, a person may be able to process visual information but cannot process auditory information at the same time. When multisensory demands are placed on this individual, sensory "jumbling" may occur.

Interestingly, individuals with adequate sensory integration turn off overwhelming multichannel input when stressed or to concentrate on a difficult task. While following directions to an unfamiliar place, the closer one gets to the destination, the more likely one is to turn the radio off in order to improve focus and decrease distractions.

Modulation is a dynamic and ongoing process. As various internal and external inputs are processed, the individual must adjust and maintain an optimum level of arousal. He must also maintain where his attention is centered.

There are varying degrees of sensory processing deficits. Within the autism spectrum, sensory processing difficulties can affect any combination of the senses in any degree of severity. Likewise, individuals with other diagnoses, such as attention deficit disorder, learning disability, Down Syndrome, traumatic brain injury, and other challenges may also experience sensory integration difficulties. The etiology of the diagnoses may be different, but the presenting sensory issues are often the same.

Communication and Sensory Integration

Kevin points for what he wants, Armond prefers to write letters, Holly uses simple signing and word approximation, and Michael speaks in complete sentences. All are communicating.

Communication is the ability to exchange information and ideas within a social setting. From the time they are born, infants begin the process of learning how to communicate. They learn to communicate by hearing, seeing, touching, and moving about their world. Infants quickly make associations between their utterances, such as crying because they are wet or hungry, and achieving the desired result—a dry diaper or food.

Essential to these communications is the complex array of sensations that alert babies to the necessity of connecting to others in their environments. From the first day of life, the accurate perception and integration of information provided by their external and internal sensory receptors give children the means to make sense of their environments. A well-integrated sensory system becomes the vehicle for nonverbal expressions, such as gestures, smiles, or frowns;

and later, for the production of speech and language. Children who experience difficulty integrating and interpreting a world full of sensations will have difficulty learning how to communicate. Without adequate processing of internal and external sensory cues, children with sensory integration dysfunction lag behind in their early communication attempts.

An individual must follow and understand not only another's speech, gestures, facial expressions, and body language, but also the context, environment, and situation being referred to by the speaker. This requires that a person process and integrate a multitude of information almost simultaneously. This is very difficult and almost impossible for the child with autism and sensory dysfunction.

Children and adults with sensory integration dysfunction experience difficulties in some or all areas of communication. Their inability to comprehend (receptive language) can be a problem, as well as their inability to express themselves verbally and non-verbally.

Accurate receptive language involves processing what a person hears when trying to understand another person. For example, a child that is hyper-responsive to sound may tune out a speaker. If he is mono-channeled and can only process one sense at a time, then listening to the teacher in a classroom setting may be impossible because of distracting movement in the room—other students too close to him, students touching him periodically, etc. An adult with mild auditory issues told a speech therapist that in a noisy setting he would resort to lip reading. Some individuals, when under stress or are tired or ill, lose their ability to process what they hear. For individuals with sensory integration dysfunction, one can only imagine the amount of information that is never captured due to difficulty in processing.

Expressive language requires the ability to mechanically produce numerous sounds and sound combinations, know the meaning of countless words, and know the rules of how these words go together (grammar) to form negatives, questions, and complex sentences. Proficient communicators also communicate non-verbally by using body language, facial expressions, and culturally accepted signs (such as waving and pointing) to convey information. Typically when we refer to language, we mean that which is verbal. However, sign language is also a recognized language. It fulfills these requirements and has its own vocabulary and rules for putting words together in a systematic way.

Children with ASD and sensory integration dysfunction frequently exhibit echolalic speech. They repeat what is said. Even though this is a typical stage of speech development that children go through as they learn to speak, echolalic speech often remains well after it is chronologically appropriate for the child with autism. Echolalic behaviors range from the repetition of sounds to words, phrases, or entire scripts previously heard. For some individuals, echolalic speech remains the primary source of communication.

In his work, *Communication and Language Issues in Autism and Pervasive Developmental Disabilities: A Transactional Perspective,* Dr. Barry Prizant delineated a hierarchy of echolalic behavior. Dr. Prizant says that a child may initially repeat, without comprehension, what he has heard immediately after a model. This may be followed by the child repeating, with understanding, either immediately after or in a delayed fashion. For example, one can ask a child, "Do you want juice?" and the child's response is, "Do you want juice?" Mitigated echolalia occurs when the child is able to alter and personalize what has been modeled. For example, you may ask a child, "Do you want juice?" and he responds with, "I want juice."

An individual may produce stereotypic vocalizations/verbalizations—speech that is said over and over. These utterances can consist of repetition of sounds, words, phrases, and even longer scripts like jingles, commercials, and videos. A person may do this for a variety of reasons. Individuals may use utterances to calm themselves when stressed, to use as a self-prompt when they execute an activity, or to block out painful stimuli.

The study of language includes the functional aspects of communication: when, how, and why. Whom do we tell when we are not feeling well—a stranger on the street, a parent, or the doctor? How do we know when we are beginning to bore the listener with our conversation? The social aspects of language remains one of the most difficult areas for individuals with sensory integration dysfunction to master because they must be able to process even the subtlest of cues. At the most severe end of the spectrum, some individuals with autism do not know that speech is used for communication.

Inappropriate pitch and intonation patterns may occur in many children. For some children, perhaps as the result of faulty auditory processing, speech may sound very robotic and monotone. For others, their speech may exhibit a highly exaggerated intonation pattern similar to the ones used in commercials or cartoons. This may be the result of speech that is echolalic in nature, and the child is repeating "exactly" as it was heard.

Accurate body awareness, and in turn, motor planning or praxis, impacts communication on many levels. From a gross motor perspective, how can a child learn to wave when he lacks body awareness and may not even know that he has an arm?

Specific oral issues can range from mild to severe. The integration of the tactile and the proprioceptive senses is necessary for an individual to be able to adequately plan and execute the various sounds needed for speech. The speed with which sounds are produced, the pressure of the lips, as well as the appropriate location of placement of the tongue and lips, are only some of the variables that are affected when these senses are not functioning optimally.

In summary, sensory integration deficits like poor body/oral awareness, attention difficulties, and high levels of arousal directly impact an individual's ability to communicate. At its most basic level, one must have good self- and body-awareness in order to use his or her body for communication.

Ryan

Ryan, a two-year-old, nonverbal child, uses position to express a limited number of needs. He stands by the refrigerator to let his mother know that he wants something to eat and stands by the front door to indicate he would like to go for a walk. He does not point for wanted items, clap hands to convey enjoyment, or wave.

The therapist encouraged Ryan to wave good-bye, by imitation as it naturally occurred at the end of each session. Despite many weeks of modeling a wave, Ryan did not catch on. The speech therapist tried using physical prompts by holding his arm firmly and waving, providing increased proprioceptive feedback. Immediately, Ryan looked at his arm as if he were aware of it for the first time.

Chapter Two
Sensory Processing Difficulties

An overview of each sensory system, including associated difficulties and behaviors, provides essential information needed prior to intervention planning. At times, the observable behaviors may be the individual's only means of communication.

Vestibular System

- Provides the unconscious information from the inner ear about one's equilibrium (state of balance) and head and body movements away from, and to, the center of gravity.

- Provides a sense of security and ties us to the ground.

- Sends information to all parts of the brain.

- Receives input from body movement and movement in the environment.

The vestibular system facilitates a sustained calm, alert, attentional state. We call it the "unifying system" because it provides the foundation for the effective functioning of the other systems. The vestibular system and auditory system are closely related, and difficulties in these areas can impact speech and language development. Attention to what is being said is needed for language comprehension and speech to develop. The vestibular system helps the brain organize and process what is being said, facilitating the development of language comprehension and speech. Slow, linear movement is calming; fast movement is stimulating/arousing.

Individuals who have difficulty with vestibular input may under-register sensory input, over-register sensory input, or display evidence of both. Behavioral manifestations of vestibular under-registration include seeking increased movement (e.g., pacing, spurts of running, rocking) or an entire lack of awareness of the vestibular input.

Under-registration of vestibular input also impacts posture, which often results in "floppy" or low tone. Observable behaviors include leaning on objects like walls for support, slumping at a table, or using arms for support during transitional movements (such as rising from a chair or the floor). A person expends much energy to compensate for decreased tone and lack of body support.

The vestibular system facilitates coordination of eye and neck muscles to adjust for head movements. Decreased registration of vestibular input impacts the coordination of eye, head, and body movements. We need this coordination to develop refined motor skills, such as writing or catching a ball.

Individuals who have low registration of vestibular input often crave movement in order to achieve an optimal level of arousal. As mentioned previously, stereotypic-seeking behaviors include rocking, impulsive running, spinning, and pacing. Movement may also be due to difficulties with balance reactions, such as maintaining sitting posture on a classroom chair.

Over-registration of vestibular input is often referred to as gravitational insecurity, or fear of movement. These individuals often have an exaggerated fear of falling and exhibit difficulty walking from one surface to another. A pause when going from grass to concrete or from a carpeted area to one with tiles is a clue. Gait may be affected: Walking with a shuffling gait allows the individual to keep both feet on the ground.

These individuals feel most comfortable with as little head movement as possible. We may observe them keeping their neck and head rigid during tasks such as eating. Avoiding tasks that require looking down and up, such as copying from a board or playing cards, is common. We may be taxing these individuals if we put them in a position that requires a lot of head movement.

In both of these cases of vestibular difficulties, the individual tends to manipulate the environment. One individual finds it more comfortable not to move, and the other is moving like crazy and not getting much out of it.

Postural insecurity is another term often used to describe fear of movement. There is a distinction between gravitational insecurity and postural insecurity. The individual with postural insecurity is fearful of movement because he lacks his own external supports—often due to neuromuscular issues like cerebral palsy. However, once positioned correctly and provided with the needed support, the individual tolerates and may even enjoy movement. The individual with gravitational insecurity, on the other hand, has the neuromuscular supports and yet does not tolerate movement.

Saul

> *At first glance, Saul, a seven-year-old with a diagnosis of autism, appeared to demonstrate motor skills appropriate for his age. He could walk on a balance beam, climb, and jump like any child his age. Further observation revealed Saul's slightly low tone. He exhibited a slumped posture*

and preferred sitting on the floor to sitting on a chair. Saul "crashed" or collapsed onto the floor during transitions. He required his arms for support when rising from the floor. He lacked the ability to maintain a workable sitting posture without keeping one hand on the floor for support, which in turn limited his bilateral hand skills. Functionally, Saul used an enormous amount of energy for simple tasks. He exhibited under-registration of vestibular input.

Alex

Alex, a nine-year-old boy with a diagnosis of autism, was referred to occupational therapy for a handwriting problem. His teacher said that Alex was able to write dictated spelling words accurately when performing these tasks at the blackboard. However, these skills were lost when Alex had to spell the words and look at the teacher while seated at his desk. Additionally, the teacher reported that when she spoke to the class from her desk, Alex was able to attend for most of the discussion. However, when she lectured while moving about the classroom, his attention was replaced with self-stimulating behavior (hand flapping). It was evident that Alex over-registered vestibular input.

Vestibular input is received not only from one's self but also from environmental movement—like the movement of others. When observing his teacher moving about, Alex used hand flapping to tune out the uncomfortable sensory input.

Proprioceptive System

- Provides unconscious information from muscles and joints.
- Gives information about movement and changes of position in space and the pressure and stretch of our muscles and joints.
- Provides body scheme/awareness.

Proprioception is our "internal eyes" and the sense that provides body scheme, which in turn allows for accurate motor planning. Accurate motor planning involves:

- **Ideation**: The conceptualizing of an idea or concept.
- **Planning**: The ability to internally organize how to move, know the sequence of actions and timing needed, and visualize the end result. Visualizing or knowing what the end result of an action will be is known as "feed forward."
- **Execution**: The ability to perform the purposeful action within one's environment. Proprioceptive input also provides the needed feedback during (and following) an action.

We receive proprioceptive information when muscles contract and stretch and joints bend. This sense facilitates smooth movements by providing information about where one's body begins and ends and about one's location in relation to the environment without constant visual cuing. Examples of proprioceptive tasks performed without visual monitoring include gesturing, pointing, and writing.

When writing, proprioception provides a sense of the pressure applied to the pencil point so that one does not press too hard or too lightly. Proprioceptive input during writing also enables the hand to guide the pencil's movements along the paper and provides feedback from the hand as to where it is in space. When we write, we look at what we are writing; we do not visually monitor our hand and arm movements. Writing difficulties can include breaking of pencil points and difficulty in forming letters and words.

Gross, fine, and oral motor skills are impacted by proprioceptive difficulties. The individual with proprioceptive issues may appear clumsy and bump into things. He may lack the skills to accurately judge the distance between himself and a wall and catch his shoulder in a doorway or going around a corner. One may observe a child who has difficulty positioning himself squarely on furniture, which in turn affects tabletop tasks as he attempts to balance himself.

Poor processing of proprioception often limits an individual's repertoire of motor skills, hindering effective interaction with the environment. Issues with self-help skills like dressing may occur. Clothing management may be difficult because we need to have accurate body awareness to arrange clothing appropriately.

Oral motor difficulties may occur, which can impact speech and/or feeding. The individual who does not know where to place his tongue in his mouth will have difficulty forming sounds and words. Inaccurate tongue movements during feeding may result in a poorly formed food bolus and cause choking.

Proprioception is stimulated through deep pressure touch and by heavy work patterns such as pushing, pulling, or carrying. Proprioceptive input is calming; therefore, in an effort to calm themselves, individuals may engage in proprioceptive seeking behaviors, such as rubbing or banging their hands together, pushing into others and objects, stuffing food, mouthing non-edibles, and grinding teeth.

Tactile System

The tactile system is the sense of touch: There are tactile receptors on the skin and inside the mouth that respond to all types of touch. The receptors allow accurate interpretation of light touch, pain, temperature, and pressure. Integration of the tactile system, along with the vestibular and proprioceptive systems, allows accurate speech articulation. Light touch is alerting—firm or pressure touch is calming.

The tactile system requires constant stimulation to keep oneself organized and functioning. Tactile input is ongoing, either through actively touching or being passively touched. There are two types of tactile systems: one is responsible for exploration, learning, and discrimination, and the other is responsible for defense. The defense system protects us from dangerous touches like sharp objects or temperature extremes. Individuals who do not process tactile information effectively may also not have an accurate awareness of temperature and pain.

Over-registration of tactile input, often referred to as tactile defensiveness, occurs when nonthreatening touch is perceived as threatening. When one over-registers tactile input, the defensive system "kicks in" rather than the system used to explore and discriminate. One may seek his space and appear fearful or angry when approached. When he is in close proximity to others, he may hit or push in an effort to increase his personal space.

Resistance to self-help skills is common. Grooming tasks, such as brushing teeth, washing one's face, and brushing hair, can all be painful experiences for the individual who is over-registering tactile input. There may be discomfort with clothing with certain fabrics, new clothing, and seams or labels. Clothing touching one's body may cause fidgeting and discomfort when sitting in a place too long. As a child becomes an adolescent, undergarments such as bras can be an issue. When touched, the individual may rub or scratch that body part. A preoccupation with cleanliness can occur.

The mouth may be sensitive, and independent feeding skills can be delayed. Going from a liquid to a solid diet could be difficult. The individual may refuse to use certain utensils or try new foods due to texture or temperature issues.

Avoidance of tasks may delay motor skill development. For example, an individual may not want to hold a pencil or have his hand rub on the paper when writing. He may avoid gross motor activities that involve contact, such as kicking or catching a ball. Sensitivity to extreme temperature or weather may cause agitation or fear, hindering one's desire to go outside. Feet may be sensitive and impact one's gait. In an effort to avoid tactile input, a person may walk on tiptoes. Over time, this can cause orthopedic issues like shortening of the heel cords.

Cal

> *Cal, a four-year-old boy, was referred for an occupational therapy evaluation due to delays with fine motor skills. Age-appropriate manipulative skills, such as the ability to copy simple strokes or snip paper, were not emerging. During the evaluation, it became obvious that due to tactile sensitivity, Cal avoided these tasks, as well as others that required tactile exploration. A program to address his tactile defensiveness included activities that provided proprioceptive input to override his heightened tactile system and vestibular input (like slow swinging) to facilitate a calmer level of arousal. Subsequently, as Cal's tactile defensiveness decreased, the therapist observed greater exploration of manipulative tasks. Cal's fine motor skill deficits resolved. Once able to hold the pencil, without the painful effects of over-registration of tactile input, Cal was not only able to imitate simple strokes but was also able to write his name and that of his classmates independently!*

An individual who under-registers tactile input may display either a decreased awareness of, or a tremendous need for, tactile input. He may have a high tolerance to pain, unwittingly injuring himself. The individual may seek tactile stimulation through mouthing objects or placing hands in the mouth. The individual may constantly rub or touch objects or people (or touch himself inappropriately). Poor tactile feedback may cause delayed, decreased, or sometimes a complete lack of response to tactile input.

Jeff

> *Jeff, an eighteen-year-old with autism, craved touch. He manipulated objects by rubbing them until his fingers bled. Jeff was unaware of pain and was known to place his hands on a hot burner.*

Accurate tactile feedback from the articulators (lips, tongue, and cheeks) allows for the production of clearly articulated speech. Oral feedback that is inaccurate hinders one's perception of the location, degree of pressure, and speed with which articulators function within the mouth, resulting in poorly produced speech.

Auditory System

The auditory system is the hearing sense that allows accurate interpretation of speech and environmental sounds. It is closely associated with the vestibular system. Soft voices are calming—loud noises are alerting.

Normal hearing acuity does not guarantee speech. A person must be able to attend, process, remember, and interpret sounds. The vestibular system is housed within the inner ear, and it is the integration of the auditory and vestibular systems that is needed for accurate processing of auditory information. In other words, it is understanding what is being said and ultimately learning to speak. Stimulation of the vestibular system directly impacts the auditory system and language. It is not uncommon to note an increase of vocalizations when the vestibular system is stimulated through swinging and rocking.

Under- or over-registration of auditory input can impact a person's functioning in many ways. In *Asperger's Syndrome*,

Dr. Tony Atwood describes noises that some people feel as intense. These include sudden, unexpected noises, such as a dog barking or a phone ringing; high pitched, continuous noises like small electrical appliances; and confusing, complex sounds like the sounds in a shopping center.

"Super hearing" refers to individuals who are unable to filter out extraneous noises such as a refrigerator running, a clock ticking, or the sound of students walking in a hallway. Loud places like lunchrooms, echoing rooms, crowded hallways, and shopping malls may cause an increase in one's level of arousal. The sound of wind or rain may make the outdoors unbearable.

Wes

> Wes was a very social young man who enjoyed people and loved talking on the phone. However, getting him to leave the house was a constant chore. The wind was so painful for Wes that he needed to wear a hooded sweater, even in warm weather, to protect himself from the sounds of even the lightest breeze.

Self-care skills, such as washing one's ears or getting haircuts, may be problems. The sound of running water can cause discomfort and result in toilet training delays or other bathroom issues. When auditory input becomes too intense, the individual may use his or her own voice to tune out the painful input. However, there can be a fine line between the behavioral manifestations of over- and under-registration of auditory input. Vocalizations can also be due to seeking auditory input or as way to provide tactile stimulation in the mouth.

Individuals may also cover their ears, grimace from sounds, or tune out all sounds to the point that they appear as if they are deaf. Appearing as if one is deaf may be to under-registration of input, as well as tuning out the input due to the perceived intensity (over-registration).

Pamela II

Here are two e-mails from Tammy G. regarding her daughter Pamela's eating difficulties:

> *I had an interesting cyber conversation with a very high-functioning gentleman with autism. I asked him if he had any idea why Pamela hates to use utensils. He suggested that it might be the noise of scraping silverware against a glass dish. So we switched to plastic. He also suggested I explain why we use utensils as he finds it hard to accept things that seem to have no purpose. I did. I told Pamela she is a big girl now, and if she eats like a baby, people won't know how smart she is. It may be my imagination, but I did not have to spend the whole meal correcting her. We'll see what develops over the next few days!*

And then...

> *Pamela no longer resists using utensils. She even puts a spoon in one hand and a fork in the other. She never seemed to "get" that before, and she started doing this on her own because the clanging noise is not there. (Pamela now uses all utensils.)*

When learning a new task, the interventionist needs to decrease other distractions. Once the task is learned, reintroduce environmental stressors because they are easier to tolerate without the demands of learning a new task.

Visual System

Vision is the process that enables a person to make sense of what is seen. Minimal background stimulus is calming. Excessive background stimulus is arousing.

Integration of visual stimuli with other sensory input is necessary for an accurate understanding of what one sees. Poor modulation of visual stimuli may result in "super vision" due to a lack of ability to block out or filter unnecessary stimuli. Increased agitation may occur in environments with multiple stimuli.

Individuals may seek visual input through self-stimulating behaviors, such as waving their hands in front of their eyes. Individuals may spend long periods of time staring into the sunlight, which can create a "break" from environmental stressors, but the behavior has the potential to cause damage to the eyes. Although these individuals possess accurate visual acuity, at times they may act as if they cannot see or may even look through people.

Olfactory System

Olfactory receptors located in our nose allow for the sense of smell. Smell and taste are closely tied. Soft and mild odors like vanilla are often calming; however, all odors have the potential to be alerting.

A person who demonstrates difficulties with the olfactory system may find any environment overpowering. Observable behaviors may include obsessive smelling or extreme aversive reactions to substances.

Bill

Incense, used during a church service, caused Bill to be physically ill and vomit.

Oral/Feeding Difficulties

Robert, a two-year-old boy, would not eat his favorite bread if it were "torn." Leonard, a sixteen-year-old, would stuff an excessive amount of food in his mouth. Cory, age one, held his lips in a tight pucker for 20 minutes following any feeding interventions. One four-year-old's diet consisted of a limited assortment of foods that could only be eaten at room temperature. All of these feeding difficulties were due to sensory integration dysfunction.

Feeding issues related to sensory integration dysfunction are mainly issues of quality rather than neuromuscular or structural difficulties that may interfere with swallowing or the mechanics of eating. The complexities of the sensory issues have the potential to cause significant health issues and render this problem area one of the most difficult to work with.

In order to simplify the task of addressing this issue, the authors have designed this chapter by dividing the following behaviors according to the sensory system. Two types of oral sensory dysfunction, "hyper" (over-registration or defensiveness) and "hypo" (under-registration) are noted with the understanding that there can be numerous other variables that may impact individuals.

Individuals with sensory integration-based feeding difficulties often deal with numerous other issues. The sensory input within the oral mechanism and characteristics of the food directly impact them. External environmental events and internal vestibular and proprioceptive issues indirectly impact the individuals. The therapists must assess and address all of these during feeding treatment. As with other sensory integration issues, oral motor problems can range from mild to severe.

The following is a sampling of possible behaviors.

The letters in parentheses indicate over (O) and under (U) registration.

Gustatory/Taste Disturbances

The individual reacts to the taste of certain foods

- Extremely selective eater (O)
- Eats only strong-tasting or bland-tasting food (O)
- Does not distinguish foods (U)
- Pica—puts non-food items in mouth (U)

Proprioceptive/Tactile Disturbances

The individual reacts to the feel of a substance and to the pressure within the oral cavity.

- Eats only soft foods (O)
- Does not chew (O)
- Too easily elicits gag reflex (O)
- Avoids certain textures (e.g., grainy) (O)
- Avoids finger feeding (O)
- Is over- or under-sensitive to food temperature
- Stuffs food (U) (Stuffing of food is normal to age 18 months)
- Grinds teeth (U)
- Has hands always in mouth (U)
- Seeks only crunchy or chewy foods (U)
- Has a preoccupation with playing with food (U)

Infants may exhibit poor sucking and/or rooting abilities. They may fall asleep as soon as hunger pains subside, following only a short period of sucking. Difficulty in transitioning to table food can occur in early childhood.

Auditory/Hearing Disturbances

- Resistance to eating due to sound produced while chewing (O)

Olfactory/Smell Disturbances

- Overreacts to non-noxious smells (e.g., gagging) (O)
- Smells food prior to eating (U)

Visual Disturbances

- Insistence on sameness (e.g., color, shape)

Chapter Three
Sensory-Based Behaviors

Sensory Defensiveness

When I was an infant, my senses didn't work right and my response to light, and sound, and touch, were not just meaningless but too acute. I could not only not understand the world, but I also could not stand it.

> Donna Williams,
> *Autism: An Inside Out Approach*, 1996

People with sensory integration difficulties frequently show signs of sensory defensiveness and react negatively or with anxiety to sensory input that is generally considered harmless or nonirritating to other people. Individuals who over-register sensory information experience sensory defensiveness.

Sensory defensiveness occurs in one or several sensory systems. It is a painful and uncomfortable experience and can impact the ability to attend and participate in life tasks. An individual can perceive voices as aversive—comparable to the sound of nails on a blackboard. A simple touch on the hand may feel like hot coals. Even the memory of an aversive experience can trigger physical distress.

Peter

> *Peter, a two-year-old with severe tactile defensiveness would physically gag and cry at the sight of a can of Funny Color Foam, a soap for children, because of the bad memory of touching it previously.*

The severity of sensory defensiveness ranges from mild to severe. The individuals with a mild impairment may be considered "picky;" they avoid unpleasant experiences. When confronted with an aversive situation, they deal with it, but they use an increased amount of energy.

Several areas of life, like self-care tasks or social interactions, can be affected for those with moderate sensory defensiveness. For those individuals, addressing and treating their sensory defensiveness enables them to participate in life experiences.

Severe sensory defensiveness affects all aspects of life. These individuals typically have other diagnoses, ranging from autism to tuberous sclerosis, in addition to sensory integration dysfunction. Appendix A includes additional information about a variety of conditions that may involve severe sensory defensiveness.

Treatment of sensory defensiveness facilitates a more appropriate level of arousal and allows increased exploration of the environment. For those severely affected, reduction of sensory defensiveness allows the therapist to treat other areas of concern, like communication, motor skills, socialization, and academics, in order to enhance the quality of life.

Self-Abusive and Self-Stimulating Behaviors

Self-abusive behavior—the attempt to injure oneself—is almost always in response to stress. Noise, visual stimuli, or the movement of others in the environment may all be too much for a person with sensory defensiveness. The interventionists may consider the environment as appropriate, but individuals with sensory processing difficulties may not be able to tolerate it.

Engaging in self-abusive behavior allows blocking out the painful environmental input. Less frequently, particularly if the behavior is new, self-abusive behavior may indicate illness. Head banging can be an indication of an earache, toothache, or headache. One report describes an individual with autism who banged his head to "get the pain out."

Repetitive, stereotypic, self-stimulating behaviors may also be the result of sensory defensiveness in an attempt to calm and gain relief from the painful stress of the stimuli. Additionally, poor motor planning skills limit many of these individuals' repertoire of movement. One can also observe self-stimulating behavior when the individual is not engaged in purposeful activity. This can be likened to "finger tapping" or "doodling." Dysfunctional, self-stimulating behaviors, often evident when an individual is not engaged, frequently diminish when the individual is engaged in a motivating task.

Edward

Edward, an eleven-year-old boy with autism, presented numerous, self-stimulating, ritualistic behaviors. Dropping plastic bottles off counters, smearing gel type substances like liquid detergent on his body, and hand flapping were only some of his frequently observed behaviors. When Edward was engaged in play on the trampoline with his brother, he was entirely different. He was attentive, followed cues, and stopped self-stimulatory behaviors.

Prompt Dependency

Children with sensory integration difficulties who exhibit poor body awareness are frequently unable to independently complete motor tasks. They become easily dependent on others to help with task completion. When attempting to teach a skill, therapists frequently use physical prompts or passive movement, such as hand-over-hand assistance, to "take one through" the motor action.

Taking one through a motor action rather than encouraging independent performance hinders the development of coordinated actions and active movement. This results in prompt dependency, or reliance on an external cue (e.g., a therapist) in order to complete a task.

Accurate processing of visual and proprioceptive information (internal and external "eyes") facilitates the development of coordinated movements or motor planning. Active, independent movement is critical for integrating these two senses and can only be achieved by decreasing physical prompts or passive movement. Use physical prompts as infrequently as possible. Always allow for the opportunity of even partial, independent performance.

Reverse chaining (allowing the individual to complete the last part of a task) while gradually expanding the motor demand is one way to decrease assistance and foster independence. For example, when working on self-feeding and hand-over-hand assistance is initially needed, remove support when the spoon is just about to reach the child's lips.

When possible, change the position of the provided physical support from direct control to indirect control. For example, during feeding, when the child becomes more adept at this skill, move physical support from the child's hand (direct control) to his wrist and then eventually gently guide at the elbow (indirect control).

Gradually moving from a firm, constant touch for support to a more intermittent touch with less pressure is another way to reduce prompt dependency and facilitate independence. Use caution with soft touch if the child has tactile sensitivity. Guidance through a motor action by the interventionist placing his or her hands near the child (but not touching the child) can provide a gentle physical "barrier" and allow for "a no-hands approach."

Children can also become verbally prompt dependent; i.e., a child depends on a verbal cue to speak or to complete a motor action. For example, Matthew only greets and says "Hi" when given the directive, " Say 'Hi,' Matthew." Matthew will only wave good-bye when prompted with the verbal directive, "Wave 'Bye-Bye'."

When teaching a child a new skill, whether it be motor, verbal, or social, the first step is to ensure (as much as possible) that the skill is at the child's instructional level. For example, one cannot expect a child to learn to use complete sentences when he is just beginning to use single words, just as a child cannot be expected to run if he is just learning to walk.

While the interventionist must initially provide as much support as necessary in order to successfully accomplish the task, once the child has demonstrated the ability to produce the skill, provide practice opportunities as often as possible with as little support as possible. A good rule of thumb is to help as much as necessary—but no more.

For verbal tasks, the hierarchy of more-to-less support generally begins with full modeling. For example, the speech therapist may begin by saying the word(s) for the child to repeat (e.g., "puppy") with a visual like the object itself or a picture. The therapist progresses to saying the beginning part of the word. Eventually, the therapist directs the child to a visual prompt of a "puppy" when soliciting production of the word. Posting the picture and the word "puppy" in the child's environment provides a way for him or her to verbalize independently.

Billy

> Billy, a seven-year-old boy with significant physical and cognitive delays, had no functional language. He responded to yes/no questions by nodding his head. When we asked Billy a question that he wanted to answer "Yes," he would take his own hand and gently push his head in an up-and-down movement. This suggests that this motor action may have been taught with extensive physical prompts, which then became part of this routine. Billy was prompt dependent; pushing his own head forward had become part of nodding.

Peter

> Peter, a two-year-old boy who possibly had autism, did not use his hands as developmentally appropriate for his age in play or to explore objects. For example, he held items in his hands without manipulating or exploring them.
>
> Peter was interested in a musical form board. A musical form board is a board that can have from one to several cutout shapes, such as a circle, square, triangle, diamond, etc. When all the pieces are in the correct place, the form board plays music as a reinforcer.
>
> Initially, Peter wanted to push the form piece into the board and elicit the desired sound; however, he was unable to

figure out how to use his hands for this task. He finally accomplished this task by pushing the piece into the puzzle with his nose. Peter was only able to complete motor tasks with his hands when provided full physical assistance by the interventionist. She firmly took Peter's hand and moved it through the complete motor action. Full physical assistance was gradually decreased, and games were provided that increased proprioceptive input, such as holding Peter's hands and pulling and pushing during "Row, Row, Your Boat." Within a short time, Peter became more aware of his body and attempted to use his hands for placement of the shapes into the board.

Hierarchy of Prompts at a Glance

Motor

- Full hand-over-hand assistance
- Reverse chaining
- Direct to indirect assistance
- Constant touch to intermittent touch with decreasing pressure
- No "hands-on" physical guidance

Verbal

- Model word(s) with visual
- Partial modeling with visual
- Cue with visual
- Visual in environment

Chapter Four
Approach to Intervention

Over the years, we have identified a few basic principles that guide our approach to treatment. Understanding that working with individuals with sensory integration disorders is as much an art as it is a science drives our therapy approach.

"Science" provides ongoing information about the disorders that enables occupational therapists (OTs), speech-language pathologists (SLPs), and other interventionists to work from a sound knowledge base.

"Art" is created when interventionists read and respond effectively to subtle cues and unconventional behaviors. Knowing when to continue with a task, when to take a break, or when to create and change the format or presentation of information are all examples of the "art" in treatment.

The individual with sensory integration dysfunction must have these issues addressed because they will affect focus, ongoing attention, and learning. The treatment approach should be sensory-based, yet eclectic. Sensory integration strategies imbedded throughout the day, as needed, can easily work with other programs in which an individual may be participating.

Activities are "individual-directed and therapist-controlled." The person's interests and needs drive the tasks. However, OTs, SLPs, and other interventionists set the parameters in order to enhance learning.

Use the child's strengths and interests to motivate him or her. This will facilitate engagement, increase participation, and enhance overall quality of learning. A child who is preoccupied with letters may participate in a cutting task if letters are the objects to be cut. The individual who is preoccupied with stereotypic, repetitive dropping of plastic objects may participate in a social activity of bowling if plastic bottles are used for the task.

Learning requires active participation. Decreasing physical and verbal prompts is essential for learning because a person can easily become dependent on prompts for task completion. The integration of visual and proprioceptive input requires active movement to develop. Taking an individual through an activity with total hand-over-hand assistance inhibits motor learning.

Processing and executing tasks frequently require increased time. Interventionists should provide sufficient time for smooth transitions.

Communication among people participating in a child's education is critical. Teaming should occur across all settings, from home to school to work, etc. Parents, educators, physicians, administrators, and therapists must all come together for optimal programming and an integrated, consistent approach to learning.

Ongoing assessment and continuous observation of behaviors and responses to input are necessary so that the appropriate intervention can take place.

Therapeutic Approach at a Glance

- Combine Art and Science
- Be Sensory-Based, Yet Eclectic
- Keep it Individual-Directed, Therapist-Controlled
- Teach to Strengths
- Provide Motivation
- Encourage Active Participation
- Provide Time
- Work as a Team
- Blend Therapies and Disciplines
- Conduct Ongoing Assessments

Treatment Cycle

In order for learning to take place, one must be able to attend and maintain attention. Look at intervention as a treatment cycle that you can use throughout the day to enhance overall functioning.

- Provide sensory integration strategies to modulate an individual's level of arousal and enhance his ability to attend and prepare for learning.

- Provide a balance between calming activities and challenging tasks that require participation and response. Over time, task demands tend to raise an individual's level of arousal.

- When the individual's level of arousal becomes elevated, decrease demands and once again provide sensory integration strategies.

Provide SI Strategies → Balance Calming and Challenging Tasks → Elevation of Arousal → Decrease Challenging Tasks → (cycle repeats)

Teaming

The cooperative effort of sharing ideas, expertise, and work leads to the formation of a team. Teaming occurs at different levels, depending on the needs being addressed. Co-treatment and consultation are vehicles for ongoing communication among disciplines, with active involvement of parents and caretakers being essential in this therapeutic process. Teaming and the blending of therapies facilitate completion of a comprehensive intervention plan for the home, classroom, or residential setting.

Although the concept of teaming is not unique, experience demonstrates that effective teaming is an ongoing and always evolving process, leading to the continuous development of new techniques and strategies. Teaming facilitates communication and results in treating the individual from a holistic approach rather than a segmented one.

Team members are aware of all areas of development and their relationship to the individual's specific needs, thus facilitating functional skill development as it naturally occurs. For example, the occupational therapist becomes more aware of the communicative intent of some motor actions. The speech therapist works on communication skills while being aware of how sensory processing issues will impact a child's level of arousal. The result of working together is synergistic, as several "heads together" often elicit more creative interventions.

Working with individuals with sensory integration issues is often a long and arduous task because many areas of development are impacted. Sharing this responsibility among team members allows for problem solving and the identification of solutions to sometimes difficult issues.

At times, more hands are needed. For example, one team member may engage the child, while the member of another discipline may impact his posture. Over time, teaming becomes trans-disciplinary as different disciplines assume each other roles as needed. This allows for seizing numerous teachable moments, opportunities that often come unexpectedly! All parties gain new and necessary tools to facilitate overall development in those people with sensory integration issues.

Benefits of Teaming

- Provides a Holistic Approach
- Creates Synergy
- Shares Responsibility
- Provides More Hands
- Enhances Trans-Disciplinary Intervention
- Facilitates Seizing the Moment
- Fosters Professional Growth

Teaming with Jon and Sammi

> *Public Law 94-142 opened the doors for therapeutic services for infants and toddlers. Jon and Sammi were two youngsters who were initially served by the speech therapist. Sammi, a two-year-old, was a premature baby with residual visual impairments. Jon, also age two, had a diagnosis of tuberous sclerosis.*

In both cases, these children resisted engagement—obtaining and maintaining their attention were next to impossible. Jon spent most of his time running around the room and placing everything in his mouth. Sammi would stiffen when held. When not engaged, she would spend extended periods of time looking at the light through the window blinds or looking, at a very close distance, at the lights on various toys. Sammi also had significant feeding issues. She avoided going from one food texture to another, eating only a few, selected items. Initial therapy with both children was inadequate.

Adding an occupational therapist provided sensory integration techniques and strategies. This assisted in preparing these children for learning. The children's needs were jointly addressed from a sensory and communicative perspective. As a team, the OT and SLP were better able to impact treatment.

Armond

Armond, a handsome boy diagnosed with autism, began receiving speech therapy when he was about five. At the time, he attended a non-categorical preschool classroom. He participated in speech therapy with a group of three or four other students. Twice a week, the group would walk across a playground to the trailer that housed the therapy room. On the walk back, Armond frequently would run away from the group. The speech therapist was left in a dilemma. Should she run after him and leave the group or let him go and hope that he would arrive at his classroom promptly?

After learning about the sensory issues that affect many individuals with autism, the therapist thought that these group therapy sessions must have been terribly taxing on Armond. He had to sit close to other students and experience a noisy, visually busy, environment.

Armond is now an adult. A few years ago, a therapist asked if he recalled running away from the group; he responded that he did. Then came the big question: "Why?" The therapist expected him to respond that it was because of stress and anxiety due to an overload of sensory experiences. Armond instead simply stated, "It was so much fun."

This story serves as a reminder that as we assess individuals for sensory integration dysfunction, we must keep matters in perspective. Individuals exhibit behaviors for a variety of reasons: to get attention, obtain something, or avoid something. Other reasons may include boredom, difficulty with sensory experiences, and, of course, because "it was so much fun."

Chapter Five

Assessment

An initial evaluation serves as an introduction to an individual's overall development and function, as well as his strengths and needs. This information lays the groundwork for an effective prescriptive plan of action.

When working with individuals with sensory and communication problems, direct hands-on testing and standardized testing is often difficult or impossible to secure. The continuous transitions from task to task, time factors, and at times, difficulty with understanding the task itself, frequently result in incomplete and inaccurate information. Strategies like direct observation, interviews with significant others, communication samples, and when possible, videos of the individual in his natural environment complement standardized testing and result in a more reliable profile.

Observations across settings allow for enhanced accuracy in identifying abilities and difficulties. Ensure that observed behaviors are typical and not due to other factors like fatigue, hunger, medication changes, or undiagnosed illness. Dental issues, stomach problems, and earaches can all produce behavioral changes.

Some conditions, including those on the autism spectrum, are behaviorally defined—there are no medical tests that can diagnose these conditions. Ideally, medical and school personnel use developmental screening instruments as a first step when there are possible concerns. Filipek, et al. (1999), provide specific practice parameters for the screening, evaluation, and diagnosis of individuals within the autism spectrum. Medical information and hearing and vision screenings are necessary.

An interdisciplinary team of specialists is the ideal choice when diagnosing these conditions. The team may include medical specialists, a psychologist, an educational diagnostician, an occupational therapist, a speech-language pathologist, a physical therapist, a social worker, an audiologist, and other professionals as needed. Parents play a critical role in the diagnostic process because research findings indicate that parental concerns about a child's development are generally correct.

A strong indicator of high risk for autism is the lack of joint attention—a skill observed in children before age one. Joint attention is a group of behaviors that includes pointing, seeking eye contact, following direction of another person's gaze, and vocalizing or verbalizing to share or show interest. Other critical indicators of possible autism include lack of babbling or gesturing (waving, pointing) by twelve months, no single words by sixteen months, lack of two-word spontaneous phrases by twenty-four months (not echolalic), or loss of language or social skills at any age.

Communication

Speech-language pathologists are the primary therapists responsible for the assessment and evaluation of communication. With younger children, initial concerns typically revolve around lack of (or delays in) speech. A thorough assessment is necessary, whether the individual is speaking or not. When possible, formal testing provides information about specific areas of speech and language. Formal instruments, however, are limited in their abilities to provide information about social communication skills that are so central to autism and related disorders.

SLPs should assess receptive language or comprehension with and without the use of contextual cues. Cues, such as an interventionist extending a hand when requesting an item, may provide the needed information rather than the understanding of the verbal directive. The assessment should include the individual's ability to comprehend words and the quantity and variety of the vocabulary used. SLPs also must examine the comprehension of simple-to-complex sentences, including use of negatives, questions, and conditional statements. When appropriate, the therapist should study the individual's ability to follow conversations and understand the more abstract elements of language (like sarcasm and innuendoes).

An expressive evaluation should include how an individual communicates—from crying, to facial expressions, to gesturing, and to using sounds, words, sentences, and complex utterances. Assess why the person communicates. Note if he or she is able to imitate, question, protest, obtain another's attention, greet, answer, and express feelings. Assessment of any alternative or augmentative system of communication, like voice output devices, sign language, picture exchange system, is essential.

A spontaneous language sample, with standardized tests, may provide an approximate profile of a child's receptive and expressive language. Popular instruments include vocabulary tests like *The Peabody Picture Vocabulary Test-3rd Edition*, a norm-referenced, quickly administered, screening instrument for receptive vocabulary (ages 2.6 years through 90+) and *The Expressive One-Word Picture Vocabulary Test-2000*

Edition, a standardized assessment instrument that measures expressive vocabulary (ages 2 to18 years).

There are several receptive and expressive language testing instruments available. The *Preschool Language Scale-3* measures receptive and expressive language in children from birth through 6 years. The *Receptive/Expressive/Emergent Language Scale Revised-2 (REEL-2)* is a receptive and expressive language assessment instrument that also facilitates intervention planning for children ages birth to 3 years. The *Sequential Inventory of Communication Development (SICD-R)* assesses the communication skills of children who are developmentally functioning within the ages of 4 months through 4 years of age.

An examination of voice quality and articulation is an integral component of a thorough evaluation of verbal children. Some children with sensory integration difficulties exhibit oral motor planning issues that affect their ability to formulate and execute the complexity of oral movements required for speech. This is known as oral dyspraxia.

Sensory Motor

An occupational therapist with expertise in this area typically conducts the assessment of sensory integration/processing skills. Parent or caregiver reporting, clinical observations, and the use of commercial instruments provide a systematic way of gathering information and interpreting observed behaviors. The therapist may reach conclusions regarding the adequacy of the various systems, number of systems involved, degree of involvement, and impact the behavior has on the individual's function.

There are many formal instruments to assess sensory integration. The authors often use *Hawaii Early Learning Profile (HELP)*, *Sensory Profile*, and *Sensory Integration Inventory-Revised for Individuals with Developmental Disabilities (SII-R)*.

Hawaii Early Learning Profile (HELP) is an assessment tool that breaks down motor, self-help, and behavior regulation for children between the ages of birth to 36 months. *Sensory Profile* provides a standardized, judgment-based, caregiver questionnaire that is intended for children between 5-10 years, but it can be adapted for children 3-4 years. This tool measures a child's sensory processing abilities and its effect on functional performance in daily life.

Sensory Integration Inventory-Revised for Individuals with Developmental Disabilities (SII-R) is a screening instrument that assesses persons who might benefit from a sensory integration treatment approach. Although designed for adults, therapists can modify SII-R for children.

Specific behavioral observations should include, but not be limited to, investigating the individual's level of arousal across settings. Examine performance during play and leisure activities. Analyze the need for personal space, observe the reaction to others within the environment, and see whether there are "avoiding or seeking behaviors."

You can determine attention span and stamina by measuring how long a person remains on task. Once the individual is attending, note the ability to transition and shift attention. Assess ease of movement during physical transitions (such as moving from sitting to standing), overall muscle tone, and general posture. You can observe motor planning skills as the individual navigates the environment.

Difficulties with sensory processing frequently lead to delays in motor output and development. Conversely, difficulties with motor output may hinder sensory development. As part of a comprehensive evaluation, occupational therapists routinely investigate not only sensory issues but also the individual's efficiency in the areas of fine motor, gross motor, and self-help skills.

Formal instruments that measure motor and self-help development provide useful information regarding current levels of performance and skills that are in need of further development. There are many formal evaluations available to assess motor and self-help skill levels.

Some of the formal instruments the authors use include *Peabody Developmental Motor Scale-2nd Edition*, which measures gross and fine motor skills of children from birth to 83 months; *Early Intervention Developmental Profile (EIDP)*; and *Preschool Developmental Profile (PDP)*. The last two are assessment-based, programming instruments that provide developmental norms and milestones for children that function between the ages of birth to 35 months and 3-to-6 years respectively.

The *Beery Developmental Test of Visual Motor Integration (VMI)* assesses visual perception, motor coordination, and the integration of perception and motor coordination of individuals functioning in the age range of 2-to-19 years. The *School Function Assessment (SFA)* helps identify a student's strengths and limitations while performing school-related functional tasks. This is a questionnaire that is completed by school professionals who know the student well and are familiar with his typical performance and behaviors.

As formal testing is often not possible, informal observations during functional tasks and interviews with those familiar with the individual may be the only means of securing information about fine motor and self-help abilities. Explore the underlying issues and barriers to successful task completion. Assessing the quality of motor skills, movement, motor planning, organization of actions, and interaction with materials in the individual's environment is critical.

When assessing a person through clinical observation, continue to be aware of normal developmental levels. For example, a child does not develop a clear hand-preference for tasks requiring precision until he is three or four. Therefore, it is not inappropriate for a two-year-old child to switch hands during tasks.

Environment

The circumstances, objects, and conditions by which one is surrounded are the environment. The environment is any and all settings in which an individual finds him or herself. Individuals with sensory integration difficulties frequently exhibit atypical reactions to the environment. These reactions can be clues as to the nature of the sensory issues.

Assessing the individual's various environments provides critical information regarding strengths and needs. Furthermore, this assessment provides an enormous amount of data regarding what environmental factors support or obstruct function. Gathering this information facilitates one of the first, and perhaps the most, impacting intervention for an individual with sensory integration difficulties. See Appendix B for a guide to assessing the environment.

Summary

The best evaluation procedures include birth, medical, and developmental history, as well as clinical observations and appropriate evaluation instruments. An effective intervention program requires ongoing assessment to determine the appropriate established objectives and to revise and change them as the child grows and develops.

There are a variety of useful assessment tools that may help as part of a comprehensive assessment. You will find some of them listed in the reference section of this book.

Chapter Six

The Environment

Individuals with autism and other sensory integration disorders need strategies and tools that will enhance their ability to regulate their world and enable them to learn and participate in everyday life. Include functional and practical sensory strategies within the environment to insure availability throughout the day.

The role of therapists is to consult with teachers, staff, parents, caregivers, and, when possible, the individuals themselves. The objective is to provide interventions that will facilitate coping strategies that decrease atypical sensitivities that the individuals have. The development and use of appropriate environmental strategies require adequate knowledge regarding the process of sensory integration by all interventionists. There must be close collaboration with those extensively trained in sensory integration, such as occupational therapists. The level of supervision should vary according to the interventions being implemented and the level of expertise of all parties.

Environmental Effects on Level of Arousal

Dr. Temple Grandin describes some sensory input as painful and recommends that individuals with autism be protected from uncomfortable sensory input. If the environment is made as predictable and as comfortable as possible, the individual is better able to focus, learn, and interact. As the individual's skills and understanding improve, we hope that he or she can more readily deal with environmental stressors.

Be aware that people affect each other in the environment. How we move, how we speak, what we wear, and how we touch others impact everyone's level of arousal.

When providing any new strategy, including environmental techniques, one should encourage, rather than force, an individual's participation. The individual often may require increasing exposure to the modification. Structure and predictability are critical; therefore, changes within a familiar environment should be gradual to allow the individual time to adjust.

The effects of the environment build. One may be able to tolerate some environmental stressors for short periods; however, as the frequency, intensity, or duration continues, the stress can cause a sharp increase in one's level of arousal. Fatigue or illness may also influence tolerance levels.

Environmental Strategies to Prepare for Learning

Modifying the environment is one of the simplest and easiest tasks that professionals have found to be extremely effective in treatment. The table on the following page lists some of the more common arousing and calming environmental factors that can increase or decrease an individual's level of arousal.

We have seen that in most instances, a calm environment facilitates attention and learning. Individuals in this environment are better able to tolerate the demands of learning and functioning.

Use caution in regard to interpreting an individual's level of arousal. An individual who appears hyporeactive or in "his own world" may actually be in shutdown and not in

Environmenal Effects on Level of Arousal

Observation	Arousing	Calming
Auditory/Noise	Loud, sudden noises or voices, changes in volume	Soft voices, rhythmic music
Visual	Bright colors, excessive background stimuli	Muted colors, minimal background stimuli
Lighting	Bright or fluorescent lights	Soft, natural lighting
Room organization	Cluttered rooms	Orderly rooms, furniture positioned around periphery of room
Vestibular/Movement	Unpredictable, fast movements with sudden changes of position	Slow movements, rhythmic rocking
Tactile/Proprioception	Light touch, tickling, and unexpected touch	Pressure touch, hugging, moving against resistance
Temperature	Sudden temperature changes, temperature extremes	Neutral warmth
Odors	Strong or noxious odors (perfume, paint)	Soft odors (banana, vanilla)

need of any further stimulation. Shutdown occurs when the sensory information is so overwhelming that the individual basically tunes out any further input.

Reduce Sound Distractions

- Lower voices and decrease the rate of speech. Loud voices may get attention, but it is hard to "hang in there," especially when typical speech is perceived as shouting. This is an easy, first step to calm an individual.

> *A parent told us, "Yesterday, after attending day one of your workshops, I tried lowering my voice when my daughter was having a meltdown. It worked!"*

- Reduce sources of background noise—close doors when there is activity in the halls. Turn off noise-producing items like fans, radios, television sets, and even air conditioning units (when possible). Decrease the volume on the phone ringer.

> *At the age of ten, Pamela required a hearing screening for her school evaluation. Her appointment was on a teacher administration day to ensure a quiet environment. The audiologist's office was small and air-conditioned, with no windows. Pamela found it difficult to maintain her attention on the task. Her mother noticed that she would drift every two minutes just when the air conditioner would click on. The audiologist moved Pamela to an empty classroom. Pamela was then able to complete the screening and passed with flying colors.*

- Use carpeting and ceiling tiles to reduce sound reverberation.

- Place tennis balls at the end of each leg to decrease the unexpected sound of a scraping chair.

- Secure foam with duct tape over the speaker to muffle the classroom bell or intercom.

- Provide a portable radio with earphones in noisy areas, such as a group home dining room, school cafeteria, or shopping mall. Large earphones provide proprioceptive input while tuning out external stimuli. If the individual is distracted by the music and resists earphones, explore using soft foam earplugs.

- Form a "lunch bunch," a group of peers meeting for lunch in a quiet area. This is an excellent way of providing a calm, quiet environment while encouraging socialization.

- To decrease arousal, provide soft music at mealtimes to allow for a relaxing "dining" experience. Music that is 60 beats per minute, classical, rhythmical, or that incorporates environmental sounds is calming.

- To increase arousal for the individual who is lethargic or presents a decreased activity level, use fast, irregular rhythm music.

Billy, a youngster with a diagnosis of attention deficit disorder with hypoactivity, was unable to complete his meal within the allotted lunch period. Fast, rhythmic music increased his level of arousal and shortened the time needed for him to finish his lunch.

Reduce Visual Distractions

- Cover items like bookshelves and toy shelves with curtains when the shelves are not in use.

- Place objects in opaque containers to decrease clutter while facilitating a need to communicate by asking for wanted items.

- Remove or turn over visuals (like circle time posters) when not in use to decrease visual clutter.

- Provide a study carrel, or use screens like poster exhibit boards on a student's desk.

- Avoid excessive wall decor and displays that hang from the ceiling and flutter. These are distracting and increase one's level of arousal. The same is true of the interventionists' clothing, jewelry, and hair. Bright or busy print clothing, hanging jewelry, and long hair can all be distractions.

> *A parent told of her child's distraction with the university logo shirts her tutors wore. The parent provided long black shirts for the tutors to wear; this simple modification enabled the child to pay better attention.*

- Keep classroom boards clean, displaying only what is immediately relevant.

- Use consistent color without patterns on the walls and floors.

- Ease visual orientation by using contrasting colors, such as a dark mat on floors in front of a light shower or commode. Contrasting colors during academics, such as placing a dark-colored paper under a worksheet, can improve the child's focus.

Lighting

Bright lighting and fluorescent bulbs often increase arousal level. The interventionist should be aware of his own position in relation to the outside light. Sun glare may cause difficulty for someone who is light sensitive, hindering his ability to maintain focus and attention. An individual who is light sensitive may benefit from sunglasses both indoors and out.

- Turn off unnecessary lighting.
- Use soft, natural sunlight and lamps with low-wattage bulbs.
- Cover fluorescent lights with swag sheeting.

Room Organization

- Keep rooms tidy and orderly.
- Use dividers to define work or play areas; when possible, use an area for only one purpose.
- Arrange furniture around the periphery of a room. Poor sensory integration frequently affects motor planing, and this arrangement improves the ability to navigate by reducing visual demands.

Manage Vestibular Input and Movement

- Be aware of your movements and slow down—fast motion is stimulating to others.

- Speak to individuals at their eye level rather than having them look up or down at you. This facilitates communication because the individual can see the speaker's facial expressions and gestures.

- Consider limiting the need for individuals with vestibular issues to travel up and down stairs. When climbing stairs is unavoidable, travel when other environmental stressors are less.

> *Wes was a thirteen-year-old boy with developmental delays and significant sensory issues. He loved working on computers, so his teachers did not understand why he did not want to go to the computer lab. They soon discovered that the road to the lab was paved with steps. By allowing Wes to go and come from lab a few minutes before the other students changed classes, other stressors were decreased, and Wes could deal with the arduous task of going up and down the steps.*

- Secure any flowing curtains.

- Explore alternative seating (e.g., a rocking chair) to provide vestibular input.

Manage Tactile and Proprioceptive Input

- Avoid very light touch because it will increase arousal.

- Approach an individual from the front rather than from behind so that he can see the touch coming.

- Touch the individual firmly for brief periods of time. Never force touch.

- Be consistent with where you touch an individual; predictability may help tolerance.

- Provide space for the individual. The end of a line, eating at the end of a table, and carpet squares during circle time may all provide needed space.

- Make alternative seating available. This can provide calming proprioceptive pressure touch throughout the day.

- Wash new clothing prior to an individual wearing it. The softer the clothes, the more comfortable they feel. Labels and seams may be irritating. Cut out labels and let individuals wear socks inside out when appropriate.

Temple Grandin reports, "It took several days for me to stop feeling a new type of clothing on my body; whereas a normal person adapts to the change from pants to a dress in five minutes. New underwear causes great discomfort, and I have to wash it before I can wear it. Many people with autism prefer soft cotton against the skin. I also liked long pants, because I disliked the feeling of my legs touching each other."

Make biker's shorts, tight sport shirts, or similar clothing to provide pressure touch to an individual who seeks this input.

Install a hand-held showerhead at home to allow more control over the water.

Control Temperature and Odors

- Provide blankets for calming, neutral warmth.
- In cooler climates, the addition of flannel sheets can provide neutral warmth.
- Avoid using plastic coverings on seating.
- Use sheepskin on chairs or mattresses as appropriate.
- Be aware of environmental odors and the individual's reaction to them. Adverse odors may come from food, cleaning products, classroom supplies, or toiletries. Use unscented products.
- Do not wear perfumes or colognes.

> *A young woman with autism was in an elevator filled with people going to a television taping. It was obvious that everyone had primped for the possibility of being on TV—even for a moment. However, the scents were noxious to this young woman, and she loudly remarked to her mother "It stinks in here!"*

Additional Environmental Strategies

Provide a "Corner of the World"

Everyone needs an area to "get away from it all," particularly when wanting to relax from daily stress. This can be a special room in the house, a certain sofa, or a special chair. A "corner of the world," an area with minimal stimuli, provides a retreat for periodic breaks.

Quiet rooms, a classroom reading corner, an appliance box lined with carpet squares, a small tent, or a small child's swimming pool, are a few examples. Incorporate various-sized pillows, beanbag chairs, gliders, or rocking chairs to provide calming proprioceptive and vestibular input. Eventually, the individuals may better be able to independently regulate their level of arousal by having an area to go to when needing to "chill out."

Alternative Seating

Various seating devices provide vestibular and proprioceptive input and, at times, boundaries.

- "Stuffed" Pants (See Appendix C)
- Beanbag chairs
- Soft, stuffed chairs
- Commercial air cushions
- Commercial "swim noodles" cut to provide boundaries on chair sides, and fastened with heavy-duty tape.

- T-Stools formed from two pieces of wood fastened in the shape of the letter "T" to create a one-legged stool (requires balancing skills and increases vestibular input)

- Therapy ball or large beach ball (stabilized in a shallow cardboard box to prevent rolling)

- Inner tubes (to prevent injury, cover the valve stem with heavy-duty tape)

- Rocking chair

- Hammock

- Glider

- Dycem® or nonskid material on a chair seat to provide additional proprioceptive feedback

- Thera-Band® tied between the bottoms of the front legs of a chair to provide additional proprioceptive input as a child moves his feet against the band

Kenny

> *An OT and an SLP assessed four-year-old Kenny at home. His difficulties included a high level of arousal, frequent movement about the room, and a preoccupation with lining up objects rather than playing and manipulating them. During the assessment, the therapists provided some quick environmental changes in an attempt to decrease Kenny's level of arousal and prepare him for task participation.*

This included lowering their voice volume, decreasing their speed of movement, and slowly swinging Kenny in a beach towel. A small booster chair provided boundaries.

When Kenny was ready, the therapists gave him a motivating puzzle task. The therapist held the pieces for play in order to facilitate communication and engagement. Within a short time, Kenny signed the word "more," a task he had only infrequently performed.

The therapists provided the parents with a home program, which included environmental modifications and sensory-based tasks. One such activity included play and exploration of sponge alphabet letters during bath time. This activity incorporated a high-stress academic demand in a relaxing task. Subsequently, the family reported that Kenny had lined up his alphabet sponges. He had lined them up in the correct order, had been able to identify each letter, and had even self-correct his errors. Previously, Kenny's cognition was considered questionable, at best.

Obviously, we cannot have every child participate in demanding tasks during bath time. However, by modifying a child's environment and embedding sensory-based tasks that meet his or her needs throughout the day, we can prepare the child for learning.

When prepared, relaxed, and attending, the child is able to access his knowledge and can show us his true capabilities.

Positioning, Positioning, Positioning

When you look at the environment, think about positioning of materials. Individuals with sensory integration dysfunction tend to have low muscle tone with poor trunk extension. Positioning of materials in a vertical plane or upright position can help in many ways.

For the speech therapist, placing materials in a vertical plane (rather than flat on a table) and encouraging pointing or reaching can facilitate extension of the trunk. With improved posture, speech therapy benefits include increased voice volume, improved breath control, endurance, and stamina.

From the occupational therapy perspective, not only is the postural control important, it also facilitates the development of the shoulder, arm, hand, and wrist that is needed for fine motor development. In this position (extension), the wrist is correctly aligned to develop stability, and it supports the appropriate thumb position needed for developing dexterity. This in turn facilitates arching of the hand, which is needed for skillful manipulation of objects.

When working on the floor, encourage a variety of postures, including side sitting, prone on elbows, ring sitting, and side lying while propped on an elbow. Discourage "W" sitting.

Encourage working either in a sitting or standing position with arms and hands moving against gravity. Provide an easel, slant board, or book holder. Position materials to encourage slight reaching; this enhances the development of arm and shoulder muscles, truck extension, and balance. Position objects on shelves, on the floor, or slightly out of reach.

Look at posture at desks and tables—elbows resting at about 90 degrees on table, knees and hips at 90 degrees, and legs supported on the floor. When needed, phone books or stacked carpet squares can be used as foot supports.

Environmental Visual Supports

Many individuals with autism and sensory integration disorders are visual learners. Therefore, we encourage the use of visual supports. Visual supports are concrete and static; they foster independence and responsibility, enhance self-esteem, and provide order, understanding, and organization to their often otherwise disorganized world.

Environmental visual supports include objects, pictures, symbols, and the written word. The selection of a visual support should be at the person's level of functioning and be as age-appropriate as possible. For example, a ten-year-old child functioning at a two-year-old level may do better when provided with a concrete object like a spoon to indicate lunch, rather than a picture or the written word. However, be aware that when individuals are at an increased level of arousal, abilities, overall, frequently diminish and visual information may need to be at a lower developmental level.

When introducing a new visual tool, you may need to demonstrate its use. This may initially increase the child's level of arousal. When the child is proficient, a visual organizer becomes a calming input in the environment.

Use visual supports across settings with all ages and developmental levels. Even though memory skills may appear excellent, stressors can tax functional memory, so cuing may be important. Effective visual supports decrease level of arousal, enhance ability to function, and minimize anxiety.

At the age of ten, Pamela had to present a social studies project to her class. The presentation involved multiple tasks, which included public speaking and the use of props, both of which cause stress. Pamela successfully presented to her class by using a prerecorded speech done by her. She was supported visually with a map that she pointed to as she played the tape.

Well-positioned, clear visuals are essential. Avoid confusing and vague visual information. For example, visuals placed too high or out-of-range are difficult to use. Overly decorative lettering can distract from essential information.

The following are some of the visual supports that a person can successfully use in a variety of environments:

Schedules/Calendars

Personal Schedules/Calendars

Students should have daily, weekly, and monthly schedules. When appropriate, begin with simplified schedules and gradually increase complexity. You can post the schedules on the wall, a desk, or have the students carry them.

Classroom and Home Schedules/Calendars

These give information about a day, week, month, or year. Be sure to sequence events within the calendar. Visually inform the students of changes in schedules; e.g., posting the word "surprise" can replace previously determined events. Using a photo can prepare the students for a visitor or scheduled events.

Visual Routines

Visual routines explain the sequence of an activity or task (e.g., washing hands, brushing teeth, dressing). For example, photos of clothing or sequentially numbered baskets with items of clothing in each, can facilitate dressing. You can expand this idea and use it with classroom activities (e.g., an art project). These children often learn to read by sight; labeling can facilitate reading skills and increase vocabulary.

Labels/Signs

Strategically placed labels/signs on objects facilitate understanding and the expression of needs. Here are two examples: During circle time, put a child's name or picture on a mat to identify which is his. At home, put the child's photo on the bedroom door to identify his room.

Lists

Lists are as varied as shopping lists, a list of class materials needed for the day, or a list of family and classmates' phone numbers. For beginning readers and visual learners, add a photo of each person on the phone list. Use dry erase boards or paper to easily compile written lists. Having the child use a list to retrieve needed materials, call friends, etc., facilitates independence.

Sensory "Cheat Sheet"

A sensory "cheat sheet" is a visual list of activities, categorized according to the provided sensory input. Post it as a quick, effective reference for both the individual and caregiver. Activities should be specific for the individual and easily embedded within a daily schedule.

Bulletin Boards

Bulletin boards incorporate finished products of activities that a child is going to participate in during school. For the older student or adult, bulletin boards announce current or upcoming events, community activities, and daily menus.

Color Coding

The use of colors can clarify and organize one's environment. Supplies needed for a specific class may be easier to access when they are all coded with the same color. For example, all of the supplies needed for art class might be coded blue.

A red stop sign on a doorway can often be enough of a visual prompt to stop a student who tends to wander. This, however, needs to be used in conjunction with a green "go" sign, to indicate when the door should be opened to exit.

Sensory "Cheat Sheet"

Tactile	Proprioceptive	Vestibular
Dry Beans, Rice, or Sand	Play the Hot Dog Game	Sit in a Rocking Chair
Work with Playdough	Pull a Heavy Wagon	Run Races Around the Room
Draw with Shaving Cream	Push Chairs Under a Table	Play Parachute Games
Massage with Lotion	Wear a Weighted Backpack	Jump on a Trampoline

> *Joe, a young man in his twenties, found it hard to verbally express his emotions. He devised a color-coded system to communicate to his mother how he was feeling. Joe wrote in red when angry, blue when sad, and yellow when happy. When his mother responded, she would use the same system.*

Visual Rules

Visual rules assist the individual by allowing him to review rules of appropriate behavior as needed. Pictorial rules (e.g., "Quiet Voices, Quiet Feet, Quiet Hands.") strategically placed around a classroom is an effective way to self-monitor one's behavior. Personal rules (e.g., lunchroom and playground behavior) can be easily seen when laminated onto index cards and secured by a ring or in photos taped to a desk.

Visual Markers

These markers provide information about one's own space, activity areas, and boundaries. For example, use masking tape on a large table or an easel to delineate individual space yet facilitate working alongside peers. Strategically place furniture around the room to create boundaries of activity areas, using gates as appropriate.

Chapter Seven
Intervention

Children learn through exploration and play. During the first year of life, infants begin with object exploration. A child achieves functional play when he appropriately manipulates objects. Symbolic play is achieved when a child is able to pretend that an object represents something else. Occupational therapists and speech-language pathologists should not overlook the importance of children learning how to manipulate, construct, and pretend, as these are the vehicles to learn communication and functional life skills.

Donna Williams, an author diagnosed with autism, said in her book, *Autism: An Inside Outside Approach*, that children with severe sensory processing difficulties often exhibit functional delays rather than cognitive delays. Functional delay refers to how an individual functions in life. It is about the capacity to act upon information in the context in which it happens. It is different than cognitive delay, which is the capacity to accumulate knowledge. One can have an unimpaired capacity to accumulate knowledge (no cognitive delay) and still have a severe impairment in the ability to access and/or act upon that knowledge independently (functional delay). At times, we perceive the individual as having cognitive issues, when in reality the individual is functionally delayed.

Environmental modifications and sensory-based activities within the treatment cycle can help an individual maintain an optimal level of arousal and enhance the ability to regulate, organize, learn, and function. When individuals are ready for learning and skill participation, they often surprise us with their abilities. Expect more from individuals and do not underestimate them. Although not all-inclusive, the following strategies have worked well for the authors.

Treatment Strategy Guidelines to Facilitate Learning and Communication

Use the following suggestions as a guide, along with the therapeutic approach and the treatment cycle, to provide a sound basis for intervention. As interventionists provide activities, they have to conduct ongoing assessments to determine the continued appropriateness of strategies and revise and change them as necessary for the individual's development and growth. Choose activities that are functional and appropriate for an individual's developmental level.

Be aware of the level of arousal and prepare for the internal and external environment through sensory integration techniques. Use yourself as a tool to help the individual maintain the appropriate level of arousal.

Motivation is critical. Gradually engage the individual by using tasks that are of his interest in order to elicit participation and communication.

Self-stimulatory or repetitive behaviors can be the basis for the development of routines. Expand routines to increase engagement. With expansion of routines, try to increase function by replacing inappropriate behaviors with appropriate activities. For example, an interest in shredding paper may eventually lead to doing papier mâché. The individual who is very interested in letters can develop motor skills by cutting, coloring, and writing letters. The one who has a high interest in lights may participate in flashlight play with others.

- Initially reinforce communication attempts and then shape them over time. Acknowledge a sound with a wanted item.

- Introduce new activities slowly. Observe the child's reactions for further intervention decisions. Do not force. Encourage activities according to tolerance level. Allow more time to respond.

- Embed easily understood communication into sensory activities. This can range from gestures, to one-word utterances, to complex speech. Providing information about what is occurring (or about to occur) helps the individual maintain alertness.

- Pair sounds or words with motor actions to increase verbal output. For example, a child can be prompted to pair the word "jump" with the action while jumping.

- Incorporate areas of need (like academic and social skills) into motivating activities. For example, have the individual count blocks or read words that go with the task, etc.

"Sabotage," or the interruption of motivating activities, provides opportunities for communication. A motivating cooking task can be "sabotaged" by withholding an ingredient that requires a request. A child enjoying a puzzle needs to communicate if the interventionist holds the pieces.

Do not be afraid of "getting egg on your face." Be creative and explore new strategies. Failure provides vital information and ultimately assists creation of effective strategies.

However, be cautious when providing prompts to facilitate task completion. Prompt dependency can easily develop. When modeling words, provide sufficient time for response attempts before remodeling. For partial, and eventually full, completion of task, gradually decrease hand-over-hand assistance.

Vestibular Input Precautions

- Stop if the individual wants to stop.
- Stop if any of the following occurs: sweating, color change in skin (flushing or blanching) dizziness, staring, change in breathing pattern, yawning, or nausea.
- Be careful with individuals who have a history of seizures.
- Never maintain a high rate of speed. Slow, steady movements are calming; fast, jerky movements are stimulating.

Sensory and Communication-Based Treatment Strategies for Children

When possible, we have grouped these strategies according to their primary sensory input. The majority of items we describe are readily available or may be easily fabricated. Several activities require training and direct supervision.

Proprioceptive/Vestibular

Portable Ball Bag

- Place commercially purchased small, plastic balls inside a large mesh laundry bag (approximately 1/3 to 1/2 full). Have the child sit in the bag with the balls. Interactive play can include embedding language concepts such as in-and-out, color identification, counting, and social skills (exchanging various balls with peers).

- Have the individual reach over or up to retrieve or give a ball to a peer—this strengthens the upper body and develops trunk extension.

- Create a "washing machine" by gently shaking the balls while the child is sitting in them. This facilitates balance reactions and increases vestibular input.

- Hide various objects and have the child find and name the objects without looking. This is an excellent language activity, as well as a tactile discrimination task.

Contact Paper

Using contact paper with the sticky side up can provide a wide array of activities that are not only fun for many of the children but also provide increased proprioceptive input and momentary tactile input (for the defensive child).

Secure contact paper, sticky-side up, on the floor with wide duct tape. When the child walks on the contact paper, you need to supervise him because his balance will be challenged. Activities on this paper include:

- Walking, with or without shoes
- Walking on tiptoes
- Walking backward, wheelbarrow-walking, crawling, or "Follow the Leader" game
- Placing and removing objects and toys from paper
- Naming the objects retrieved

Art activities may include sticking feathers, crumbled papers, yarn, and other tactile materials on contact paper in order to make a collage that can be displayed after completion.

For the student who is physically challenged or just unable to manage glue, place a stencil cut from construction paper over contact paper. Encourage placement of a variety of materials to complete an art project. For example, cut an opening in the shape of a pumpkin from construction paper. Place this template over the contact paper and encourage the child to place crumbled orange tissue in the cut out shape.

Take a nature walk and make a "bracelet" of sticky-side-out contact paper. Have the children find items such as leaves, flowers, etc. and place them on their wrists. Bending and reaching for materials encourage balance skills. Encourage directionality by indicating, for example, "There is a flower on your left side." Upon completion of the project, encourage discussion of items retrieved and the sensory components (e.g., the flower is soft and smells, the leaf is green, etc.)

Towel Rocking/Pulling

Place the child on his back on a towel. Gently rock him side-to-side. You can also pull a child along the floor on his stomach or back. Singing during this activity can prepare the child for starting and stopping points and facilitates word completion. For example, "This is the way we take a ride, take a ride, take a ride…" As this is a very motivating activity, sabotaging by stopping periodically allows the child to request more. This is an excellent preparatory activity to gain attention (eye contact) and increase vocalizations.

Playground Equipment.

Swings, slides, and climbing equipment in a playground offer unlimited opportunities for vestibular and proprioceptive input. Explore various positions on the equipment, such as sliding on the stomach both forward and backwards, and swinging on the stomach.

Racetrack Play

Create a track with tape on the floor. While the child is on all fours, have him "race" a toy car while staying on the track. This incorporates weight bearing (proprioception, movement (vestibular), and eye/hand coordination. This is an excellent opportunity to embed fun sounds, like "roommm, roommm," "beep, beep," etc.

Creating a "track" in sand is an excellent pre-writing task. Have the student move an item on a path from left to right (e.g., move toy farm animals along a path from the meadow to the barn).

Obstacle Course

- Use home and classroom objects to create an obstacle course. Sofa cushions, tables, chairs, sticky contact paper, commercially available wedges, rolls, large blocks, mats, etc. are all useful. Have students create the course.

- Incorporate stories and language concepts. Include prepositions such as "over," "under," and "through" in the activity.

- Write concepts on cards and place them in appropriate spots so that the child can visually see the word, hear the word, and do the action.

- Encourage students to complete courses in a variety of positions such as walking and crawling.

- Obstacle courses provide increased proprioceptive input and develop motor planning skills.

Weighted Toys and Materials

- Play with materials that have weight. This stimulates proprioception. Stacking wooden blocks, organizing bookshelves, putting away groceries, and pulling, pushing, and carrying activities are examples of "weighted" activities.

- Add weight to some materials like cardboard blocks or empty food containers by using substances like dried beans or rice in plastic bags. Be sure to seal the bags with tape.

- Reinforce classification skills by sorting a variety of empty food containers. Add weight and tape boxes shut. Have students sort the food containers into large brown grocery bags according to set criteria, such as the freezer or refrigerator, fruit or vegetable, and healthy choice or junk food.

- Use a wagon or cart during block play and have the child deliver blocks and other slightly weighted toys to a building "site" that you have begun. Have the child load/unload and help build the house. Reinforce language concepts by pointing out changes that occur in the building (e.g., "The house is getting taller.") Following adult oral instructions enhances receptive language skills.

Fine Motor Tasks with Resistance

Hammer and peg sets, many types of pegboards (including those with lights), and puzzle pieces with Velcro® backing, all offer resistance. You can encourage social engagement by maintaining control of pieces rather than giving them all to the child. Hold pieces so the child has to reach across his body to facilitate gentle reaching, stretching, and midline crossing.

Thera-Band Activities

You can purchase Thera-Band through an athletic supply store or a therapy catalog. Nylon stockings are a substitute; however, they do not provide the resistance of Thera-Band.

- Encourage the child to hold both ends of the Thera-Band and stretch arms out to the sides—up and down.

- Place the band behind the child's back and have him pull to sides.

- Place the Thera-Band under the child's feet and have him pull up, etc.

- Encourage the child to hold one end of a Thera-Band and "squirrel" it into the palm to facilitate small muscle and hand-skill development.

This resistive activity facilitates overall large muscle strengthening. Naming body parts and position concepts enhances language skills, body awareness, and directionality.

Exercise/Group Sports

The following exercises incorporate heavy-work patterns and develop leisure skills. Vigorous exercise, twenty minutes or longer, three or four times a week, is calming. Mild exercise has no effect. (Edelson, Stephen—see References)

- Walking
- Running
- Hiking
- Swimming
- Horseback Riding
- Weight Training
- Bowling

Horticulture Tasks

These horticulture tasks involve heavy work patterns that provide increased proprioceptive input, overall muscle development, and (frequently) enhanced self-esteem when an individual finishes a product.

- Gardening
- Planting vegetables

- Raking
- Digging
- Cutting Grass
- Pushing compost barrels

Classroom/Home "Jobs"

- Pushing chairs under desks
- Wiping the dry erase board
- Carrying books to the classroom
- Stacking and sorting library books
- Pulling a wagon of toys for outside play
- Putting away groceries
- Sweeping
- Vacuuming
- Setting or clearing the table
- Emptying trash
- Washing/drying clothes
- Sorting clothes of different textures
- Folding warm clothes
- Rearranging furniture
- Washing cars
- Cleaning wheelchairs
- Sharpening pencils

- Using hole punchers
- Stapling

Massage

We recommend training before providing this program.

Frequent professional massages, or massages provided by a parent/caregiver who has been trained in infant massage, can be beneficial. The pressure touch of a massage stimulates proprioceptive receptors, which in turn, overrides a heightened tactile system and helps to modulate the vestibular system. Studies by T. Field (see References) found that children with autism benefited from massage therapy. The researchers concluded that massage therapy decreased touch sensitivity, distraction by sounds, and off-task classroom behavior.

Massage stimulates all the senses to help reinforce the learning process through tactile (touch), auditory (background music), olfactory (smell), and the tactile experience (deep pressure provided by another). This helps make the individual feel safe and comfortable, facilitating the building of a relationship. It can initiate the process of developing effective communication. With appropriate preparation, professional massage can benefit the older child or adult.

Gentle pulling and compression of the arms or legs stimulates the proprioceptive receptors in the muscles and joints. We may find that the child who is seeking this input offers his arms or legs to be gently pulled, pushed, or massaged.

Sock Massage

Placing a glove puppet or tennis sock over an interventionist's hand and then applying deep pressure strokes in a downward motion over arms, legs, and back of the individual can provide proprioceptive input. Avoid friction and continuous motion over the same area. Do not force the touch—prepare the child in advance. At times, a child with tactile sensitivities will tolerate a sock massage rather than the direct physical contact of one's hand needed to implement a massage.

Mummy Game

This activity should only be implemented under the supervision of a trained therapist

Wrap an Ace® bandage on a child's arms and legs from distal (wrist or ankle) to proximal (armpit or thigh). Apply pressure without constriction. Have the child wear it for approximately 20-30 minutes, generally 1-2 times daily. This provides increased proprioception and body awareness.

Pressure Brushing/Wilbarger Protocol

Implementing this program requires specialized training.

This strategy, a technique often used for sensory defensiveness, was developed by occupational therapists Pat and Julie Wilbarger. It is an intensive approach. Although often called a brushing program, it involves pressure touch, which stimulates deep touch receptors and joint compression that stimulate the proprioceptive receptors.

Home Activities

Bath Time

Washing can help organization. With soap on a cloth, provide a few moments of deep massage. Incorporate language and body awareness by naming parts as you wash.

- Use deep massage on the child's head prior to, and during, washing her hair.

- Wrap the child in a large towel after the bath and provide deep pressure massage while drying. Follow with long body hugs.

- Apply deep pressure massage prior to hair brushing because this may help the child who finds hair brushing aversive.

Hygiene/Grooming

- Incorporate tactile input using lotions, talc, and hair or teeth brushing.

- Massage hands and feet with a lotion.

- When using lotion, put a small amount in a person's hand and have him rub lotion into his elbow, wrist, fingers, toes, etc.

- Incorporate language by identifying body parts.

Bedtime

Tucking a child in bed, or placing pillows tucked around the top of the child's head, shoulders, back, and hips, can provide pressure touch and boundaries. Sleeping bags or heavy quilts can promote calm, restful sleep. Develop a bedtime routine and eliminate rough play (tickling, wrestling, etc.) before bedtime

Tactile

"Stuffed" Sweatshirt

Tactile exploration is a critical part of normal development. Most preschool and kindergarten classes have "tables" filled with water, sand, dried beans, and rice. Some of our students are unable to participate in this type of play due to mouthing. Using "stuffed sweatshirts" (see Appendix D) prevents students from mouthing while they manipulate small objects. It encourages tactile exploration and the development of discrimination skills.

Additionally, placed on one's lap, this tool provides proprioceptive input. Encourage exploration and hide small objects to increase interest and develop language. Incorporate vocabulary and labeling of objects.

Activities in Tactile Substances

Use water, sand, rice, dried beans, shredded paper, Easter grass, packing material, and popped/unpopped popcorn (supervise as appropriate).

- Place the substances in small containers for hand exploration and in large containers for whole body play.

- Use indoor/outdoor sandboxes, plastic swimming pools, etc. to contain different substances like dried pasta, dried beans, or balls. Hiding and finding objects in substances facilitates tactile discrimination skills.

- Writing or tracing in moist sand or dirt provides increased proprioceptive feedback.

- Hide letters and objects and encourage the individual to find the letter and then find an object that begins with that letter.

Pouring Activities

- Use large measuring cups to practice math concepts (this facilitates fine motor skills).

- Mark cups with a heavy dark line to enhance visual perception of the measurement lines.

- Practice functional precision tasks, such as pouring and measuring dried beans.

Exercise Putty and Play-Doh®

- Encourage molding and rolling putty or dough.
- Roll dough or putty into tiny balls by using only the fingertips of the thumb, index, and middle finger; or roll flatten on a table or vertical surface.
- Use small pegs or toothpicks to make a design or a plastic knife to cut dough.
- Increase interest by hiding small objects such as magnetic bingo chips in Play-Doh. This strengthens hands and fingers.
- Encourage vocabulary by putting objects "in" and pulling objects "out" of Play-Doh.

Play Dough in a Bag

This is a great activity for children who have tactile sensitivity. There are many recipes for homemade play dough. Each child can make play dough by placing the ingredients in a gallon-size, Ziploc® bag and sealing it with wide tape. Encourage manipulation, squeezing, writing letters, etc.

Here is a recipe:

1 cup flour
1/3 cup salt
1 teaspoon oil
1/3 cup water with food coloring

Mix dry ingredients and add water and oil gradually. Add more water if too thick; add more flour if too sticky.

Water Activities

At a water work area or sink, provide large basters, plastic eyedroppers, sponges, etc. Have the child squeeze these tools to fill various containers. This facilitates the development of hand and finger strength, eye-hand coordination, and encourages functional play with a variety of tools.

Put Styrofoam® packing material into water and capture pieces by using hands, strainers, slotted spoons, or other tools. Facilitate sorting skills by cutting various shapes from the Styrofoam used in the water. You can also use sponge letters, numbers, and animal shapes. Identify the letter, number, or animal captured.

Art and Finger Painting Activities

Have children finger-paint, using a variety of materials like paint, puddings, Cool Whip,® Funny Color Foam, or shaving cream. Add a drop of food color to shaving cream to add interest and encourage color identification.

- Secure a picture or drawing to a tabletop and cover with clear contact paper. Have the child "color" or cover picture using finger painting material. This can encourage the child's focus on the task.

- Practice handwriting by writing words in shaving cream.

- Teach letter sounds by placing a clear plastic board over pictures with the same starting letter. Cover with shaving cream and have the student write the letter while saying the sound. Push away the shaving cream to reveal pictures with that sound.

Sticker Play

As tolerated, place stickers on arms, hands, legs, feet, head, etc. as part of a game. This increases body awareness and identification. Placing and removing stickers on laminated paper or balloons provide opportunities for fine motor manipulation and eye/hand coordination.

Dress-Up Area

- Provide a box filled with hats, gloves, shoes, glasses, jackets, rings, bracelets, necklaces, and socks.

- Increase body awareness by using elastic bracelets and spandex tubes for arms or legs.

- Reinforce language concepts by asking the child which body part garment goes on and what he wants to put on next—have him name the item and put it on.

- Read a story, play "dress-up," and "play act."

Ball Play

In play, children can roll, throw, bounce, catch, kick, or pass a ball. Using balls with a variety of weight, size, and tactile and visual components can facilitate coordination, motor planning, and tolerance of tactile surfaces. Reciprocal ball play is an excellent means of developing social skills.

Cooking

- Mix ingredients (by hand, if possible) and knead dough. Use tools like cookie cutters, sandwich spreaders, and rolling pins. All of these tasks incorporate heavy-work patterns and fine motor manipulation.

- Make juice or lemonade and handle ice cubes.

- Follow recipes to incorporate math, reading, motor coordination skills, social skills, etc.

- Make cookie faces using icing, raisins, licorice, etc.

- For the individual who lacks motor skills, you can adapt electrical appliances with a PowerLink,® remote switching device.

Visual

Flashlight Games

Encourage the child to chase a flashlight beam or to follow it with his eyes. Ask the child to catch or step on the light. Take turns moving the light. To encourage language, ask the child to tell you where the light is by using phrases such as "under the table."

Shining a flashlight on an object, like a picture on a page or a specific toy can facilitate an individual's focus. Try using a flashlight with an adjustable beam (e.g., Maglite®).

Mirror Play

Practice songs with arm movements in front of a mirror. This may help some children see how their bodies move, where they are, and how their bodies are connected. Provide a mirror in "play dress-up" area.

Motivational Toys

There are many commercially available toys that are motivating and provide auditory, visual, and tactile input.

These toys also provide opportunities for learning and communication. Here are a few examples:

Magnetic bingo chips	Musical form board
Travel Etch a Sketch®	Puzzle: Tactile
Musical rings	Musical busy box
Musical block tower	Books: touch, feel, and sound
Travel sparkle lights	

Handwriting

Handwriting skills develop sequentially. Imitating what the teacher has written, directly following a demonstration, is the first step in writing. Copying skills then develop from near to far. Copying a letter or word on the same paper is easier than copying from a book, and copying from a book is easier than copying from a black- or whiteboard. Independent writing is the final skill.

For the adult, acquired handwriting skills can be functionally embedded throughout the day for continued learning through personal correspondence, shopping lists, "things to do lists," etc.

Positioning is essential during writing tasks. As illustrated in Chapter 6, bent elbows should rest comfortably on the writing surface at approximately 90 degrees, knees and hips should be flexed at approximately 90 degrees, and feet should rest flat on the floor. Incorrect desk posture can compromise balance, limit arm movements, and hinder accurate handwriting. Stacked phone books, held together with duct tape and placed on nonskid material to prevent sliding, can elevate a child's dangling feet and eliminate the need for the child to wrap his or her legs around the bottom of the chair for stability.

Handwriting Adaptations and Suggestions

Providing movement activities prior the handwriting practice can increase awareness of hands and fingers. Use short teaching sessions (10-15 minutes) and 5-minute practice sessions. Increase interest by having the student copy from his favorite book.

Encourage handwriting practice in the vertical plane. Working on a vertical surface enhances the development of appropriate hand and wrist positions for fine motor and handwriting skills, as well as the development of arm and shoulder muscles. Provide opportunities to work in sitting or standing positions with arms and hands moving against gravity either at the board, an easel, slant boards on a table, or other vertical surfaces. When writing on a slick surface (e.g., slant board), place the paper on top of a manila folder or ink blotter to allow for increased pencil control. Fun positioning adaptations can include writing or coloring while lying on stomach and propped on elbows. For a complete change, tape paper on the underside of a desk or table and have the child draw while lying on his back.

Observe the individual's writing grasp and encourage him or her to use the "holding hand" to stabilize the paper. When pencil grip is poor (thumb is wrapped around the pencil, for example), explore commercially available pencil grips. If the pencil is held too close to the point, wrapping a rubber band one inch above the point can provide a visual cue for finger placement.

Be aware that atypical pencil grips do not always affect one's writing legibility; rather, look at the components of writing such as using intrinsic muscles (small muscles in the hand), positioning the wrist properly, and maintaining distal control. Using crayons broken into "stubs" can facilitate appropriate pencil grip as the small piece of crayon must be held between the fingers and thumb. Provide coloring books based on individual interests.

Writing on slant boards can compensate for vestibular difficulties. Use commercially available products or make one by using a four-inch binder. You can glue a "chip clip" to the top of the binder or spray the binder with a photo-mounting spray to secure the paper.

- A strip of masking tape placed on a desk can cue a child where to place paper.
- "Handwriting without Tears," a program by Jan Olson, has been successful with many of our students.

Pamela

> *Pamela recognized all her letters; however, due to initial tactile issues, she refused to hold a pencil. The wooden shapes from the "Handwriting without Tears" program were used as an alternative, and she successfully learned how to form her capital letters without ever lifting a pencil. Eventually, Pamela began writing and continued to use this program with modifications, such as increasing the distance between the lines.*

Explore using the following sensory-based strategies as appropriate:

- Provide visual cues for writing by color coding each letter stroke for clarity (e.g., 1st stroke blue, 2nd stroke red, 3rd stroke green).

- Encourage exploring letters of various textures like plastic, foam, and wood. This allows students to "feel" the letters.

- Have the child write in pudding, sand, or shaving cream to provide tactile input. At home, you can reduce cleanup by using Funny Color Foam for writing activities during bath time.

- Have the individual form, trace, or shapes letters from clay, WickiStix,™ or cotton balls for tactile input.

- Let children trace letters or words with glue and sprinkle them with Kool-Aid. This provides olfactory input.

- Increase proprioceptive feedback by using a vibrating, weighted, or felt-tipped pen.

- Provide paper with raised or colored glue lines to cue for line usage.

- Place fine sand paper under the writing paper to increase proprioceptive input.

Additional Adaptations and Modifications

Spacing and Line Usage

- Use a decorated tongue depressor, a pencil, or one's finger as a guide— or have the student make a dot between each word to assist with spacing.

- Use graph paper to help with spacing of math problems. Turn lined paper sideways to help with letter and number spacing.

- Highlight lines to provide increased visual cues for starting and stopping points on a paper.

Copying

- Provide larger areas for writing when appropriate. Research indicates that individuals with autism tend to write larger than typical peers at the same level.

- Place work to be copied next to the student on a slant board, which is easier to read from than a horizontal surface. This modification will help students who have trouble copying.

- Use a marker (e.g., ruler, laminated colored paper strip, etc.) to keep place when copying from a book.

- Activities such as tossing bean bags or ball at a target placed at approximately the same distance as the student is from the board can provide practice focusing and fixing eyes near and far.

Attention Suggestions

- Limit environmental distractions.

- Limit peripheral distractions. Use a study carrel when appropriate.

- Use a black mat that is larger than a worksheet to assist in visual attention to the worksheet.

- Provide a surgical brush attached with heavy-duty tape to the underside of a student's desk to provide a discrete and convenient place to "fidget."

Computer Adaptations

When appropriate, computers offer an excellent alternative to handwriting as well as an adjunct to it. Computer technology changes rapidly. "Closing the Gap" (see Resources), is a resource that produces a quarterly periodical and a yearly resource guide to current technology for individuals with challenges. This is an excellent way to keep current on what is new in software and hardware.

Weighted and Pressure Touch Equipment

Weighted items are garments and other weighted objects that are worn by a child or adult to provide proprioceptive input. This often reduces an individual's level of arousal during demanding times like transitions and deskwork. See Resources regarding suppliers of weighted equipment.

Consultation with a trained therapist is essential when adding weighted items on an individual.

Weighted Vests

Weighted vests (see Appendix E) should not be used by individuals who are pregnant or who have respiratory difficulties like asthma or upper respiratory infections. We recommend that individuals wear the vests for 20-to-30 minutes and then leave them off for at least 30-to-60 minutes. One can purchase the vests pre-made or you can make them from hunting, fishing, or jean vests. Watch for possible difficulties caused by excessive weight, including drooping shoulders, difficulty in moving, mellowness, or lethargy.

Individualize the weight to each child or adult. Start with small amounts of evenly distributed weight and add or reduce weight as appropriate.

A person's size is not always an indication of needed weight. Vest manufacturers appear to recommend up to approximately 5% of a person's weight. Studies show that you should not apply more that 10% of a person's weight due to orthopedic concerns.

Additional Weighted Items

Lap Pockets

This is a device made out of cloth that sits over an individual's lap and hangs several inches below the chair seat. Use Velcro to close pockets/channels on both sides. Add weight by filling the pockets/channels with dried beans or rice. Use lap pockets during sitting tasks.

Weighted Sock

This is a long tube sock filled with rice that is securely sealed either by sewing or with a rubber band. Use as a "sitting pal" during tabletop tasks.

Blankets

During nap time, you can use beanbag chairs as "blankets." For an older child or an adult, an X-ray vest can serve as a blanket. Keep in mind the precautions regarding weight (20-to-30 minutes on and at least 30-to-60 minutes off). When visiting a dentist, you may want to allow individuals to wear an X-ray apron for the entire duration of the visit rather than only during X-rays.

Weighted Backpack

A backpack weighted with books may be help a student during transitions from class to class. Be careful to avoid excessive weight or having the student wear the backpack for more than 20-to-30 minutes.

Commercially Available Weighted/Pressure Items

Body Sock

The body sock is made from stretchable material. The individual can "get into" this sock and be enclosed from head to toe, providing pressure touch throughout. He can see through it and move somewhat while in it. The body sock can also be worn to the shoulder so that the head and face are free from cover.

Huggy Vest

This is a vest that provides pressure in the upper trunk and shoulders. A huggy, weighted vest is one that combines pressure and weight.

Weighted Hand Patch

The individual wears the patch on his or her hand, particularly during writing tasks or fine motor activities, to increase awareness.

Weighted Foot Patch

The individual wears the patch on his or her shoe to increase lower extremity awareness.

Weighted Collar

This collar, with channeled, weighted inserts, provides pressure to the shoulders.

Sensory and Communication-Based Treatment Strategies for the Adult and Older Child

Although you can modify many of the previous activities for the adult and older child, the following tasks are specifically geared for this population.

Proprioceptive/Vestibular

Can Crushing

To install a can crusher, mount it on a wooden board and attach it to a table with a "C" clamp. This allows the individual to sit while working. Can crushing encourages a variety of vocational skills like math, social, and money management (e.g., count the cans placed into bags, take the cans to a recycling center to be reimbursed, and pick up cans at various sites, etc.). This is an excellent heavy work task that provides proprioceptive input, as well as a repetitive "calming" action to complete the activity.

Ellison LetterMachine Tasks

The Ellison LetterMachine (often called the "Ellison press," see Resources) creates templates. These templates range from simple letters and forms to more extensive patterns that can be used to make pads, note cards, or boxes. The cutting of these patterns is repetitious and stimulates proprioception.

Woodworking Activities

Cutting and shaping wood, sanding, hammering, and drilling are some of the components of woodworking. Skills developed include organization, language, eye/hand coordination, safety issues, and stimulation of the proprioception through the heavy work patterns. Supervision is recommended as appropriate.

Exercise and Group Sports

Walking, running, hiking, swimming, horseback riding, weight training, and bowling incorporate heavy work patterns and develop leisure skills. Vigorous exercise, 20 minutes or longer, 3-to-4 times weekly, is calming (mild exercise has no effect). (Edelson, Stephen).

Household and Office Chores

There are many functional home, school, and office tasks that provide proprioceptive and vestibular input. Additionally, using these tasks throughout the week can enhance self-help independence, attention to task, fine motor strength, and manipulation skills. Mastery of these skills is also a great self-esteem builder! When appropriate, provide positive reinforcements like verbal praise, music, videos, etc. Options for implementation can include having an individual chose one task from two daily or posting a calendar with daily activities. Encourage discussion regarding activities for that day.

- When buying groceries, have the individuals follow a written or pictorial list, locate items in the store, and put away groceries at home. When putting away groceries, grade item weight, size, and placement on shelves at different levels to promote upper extremity strength and balance.

- Use cooking activities to develop upper extremity strength and dexterity, bilateral skills, and attention to task. Incorporate simple meal planning, such as listing items needed to prepare a recipe. Making the same item several times can help develop memory skills (i.e., what items are needed, what is the sequence, etc.). Begin with simple recipes, such as mixing pudding, Jell-O,® prepared hot or cold cereals, etc.

- Cooking activities can incorporate mixing by hand, rolling, pinching dough for cookies, and cutting fruits or vegetables with careful supervision, which provides heavy work patterns, as well as tactile input. Serve the "creations" to self or family.

- Load and unload the dishwasher, sort silverware and plates, etc. to develop attention to task and bilateral hand skills.

- Laundry tasks include carrying laundry to the washing machine, sorting, and loading into washer or dryer.. Encourage using hand-over-hand motion to remove large items from washer or dryer. Sort (e.g., towels, colors and whites, matching socks, etc.) and put away clothes. Fold clothes, grading difficulty from simple washcloths and towels to rolling socks, etc. Hang clothes on hangers to promote upper extremity strength, motor planning, and attention to task.

- Develop upper extremity strength by sweeping, vacuuming, and emptying trash.

- Set and clear the dining table to enhance attention to task and bilateral skills.

- Increase motor planning and upper extremity strength by making beds, removing linens, and placing pillows in cases.

- Rearrange, stack, or move furniture.

- Sort and stack books and magazines.

- Encourage "tearing" old mail, crumble in palm, and toss into a wastebasket. Have the individual place stamps on outgoing letters and mail them. This develops hand strength and eye-hand coordination.

- Sharpen pencils, punch holes, or staple paper. Use manual, electric, or switch-adapted equipment.

- Wash cars, squeeze sponges, and wring out rags to promote balance and hand strength.

Tactile

Sorting and Categorizing

Sorting and categorizing incorporate academics, language, and life skills development. Sorting clothing for washing, folding, and putting away; organizing silverware in a drawer; placing dishes according to size in a dishwasher; sorting and rolling coins; and organizing food in a pantry are some examples of functional tasks that can provide numerous tactile experiences.

Art Activities

Ceramics and pottery incorporate hand-strengthening and proprioceptive input to hands and fingers, as well as developing self-esteem.

Paintings and drawings make wonderful note cards or holiday cards. Reduce a large-sized picture (black and white pictures work particularly well) to fit on the front one-quarter of a colored 8" by 10" sheet of paper. Fold to make into a card and add a matching envelope. Individuals can give cards as gifts or sell them. Great self-esteem builder!

Leisure Activities with Assorted Balls

Incorporate balls with a variety of weights and sizes, as well as tactile and visual components. Encourage activities like bowling, catch, and basketball. Provide word lists, when appropriate, of the terminology we use for these sports.

Water Activities

Swimming provides increased overall muscle strength, as well as an excellent leisure pastime. Washing dishes, hand-washing clothes, showering, maintaining a fish tank, and washing a car are all functional ways to encourage exploration of water activities.

Vocational/Enterprise Activities

Several of the activities previously discussed allow individuals to experience "running a business." With adaptations and assistance, individuals can learn to run a successful retail business. Participation in "enterprise" activities vary, but participation often includes the development of many of the following:

- Self-esteem
- Academics
- Social skills

- Communication
- Fine motor skills
- Job-related attitudes and skills

Additional "enterprise" activities may include balloon sales, plant sales, and delivery services.

Transitions and Waiting

Individuals with autism and a few other disorders are frequently preoccupied with sameness. Transitions and change can be difficult for some individuals with sensory integration dysfunction. Issues with shifting attention from one task to another, moving from one place to another, and waiting are continual problems. Providing clear communication, which results in understanding, combined with appropriate sensory input, often eases transitions and waiting.

Transitions are the changes that occur regularly on a day-to-day basis, such as going to bed every night, having lunch during the school day, beginning a new endeavor or activity, having a new person in the day (e.g., a substitute teacher), or going to a new school.

Transitions can be difficult for individuals with autism and other sensory difficulties—even when the next event or situation is one that is liked and motivating. Establishing clear expectations and routines facilitates ongoing changes that occur naturally during the day at school or home. Teach a child to transition and wait by providing him with supports and rehearsing it so that it becomes a learned skill that he can apply when needed. Difficulty with waiting and transitioning prevents some students from participating successfully in inclusive school settings.

One of the most successful and easy strategies to facilitate transitioning is providing more time. A five- or two-minute warning or transition to the count of ten may be all that the individual needs.

- Establish routines and use daily schedules in the form of checklists or picture guides for the individual to follow.

- Before unexpected changes occur, decide how changes will be shown on the schedule. For example, place the word "surprise" or "change" in the schedules and present these to the individual as soon as possible.

- Prepare an individual by telling or showing (visually) where he will be going and what he will be doing.

- Let the individual feel or hold objects from a schedule board (e.g., a spoon for lunch, a car for a trip, and a toy bus for leaving school). Provide visual icons like photographs and words, as appropriate. These are commercially available from Mayer-Johnson (e.g., Boardmaker®) and other companies.

- Use music and song to indicate transition; for example, singing "The Cleanup Song" can motivate a child to pick up toys to end an activity.

- Use a transitional photo book to prepare the child for a change or an activity that might be stressful, such as going to a new school or the dentist, by providing pictures of places and people, as well as activities that will occur in this novel event.

- Dim lights to aid in transitions by providing a change in the environment and a decrease in the level of arousal.
- Provide a slow loss in room lighting to aid bedtime transition with "glow in the dark"—neon adhesives that gradually lose their glow
- Make the individual an active participant in the transition; for example: "Let's take that book to my room."
- Using a weighted vest, pressure vest, or a weighted backpack provides increased proprioceptive input as well as a visual cue to indicate transition, both of which are calming. (Please see directions and contraindications for using weighted items.)
- Encourage marching, hopping, or any type of little game during the move. This provides increased proprioceptive input.
- Provide steady, firm pressure on the top of a student's shoulder while walking alongside during transitions.
- Use timers to help an individual better understand waiting, and to provide a tangible way to conceptualize time.
- Provide a carpet square to show the child where he needs to stand while waiting for his turn at the computer or engaging in a P.E. activity.
- Provide a "waiting object" for the individual to hold during transitions, such as a textured ring, key chain, a favorite book, a can of soda, or a calculator. A fanny pack filled with assorted items provides a "fidget" and can decrease anxiety during waiting periods. Also provide a "waiting card"—a laminated index card with a symbol or picture and the word "wait."

Informational Tools

Informational tools are pictorial or written assists that provide information about an individual. The tools facilitate consistency of care and integration of services in order to enhance the person's functioning.

Transitional Photo Book

As the individual transitions to a new class, school, residence, work, etc., a transition book provides a visual introduction. This tool informs teachers, caretakers, and supervisors about the individual's needs and strengths. It describes present levels of skills and lists favorite activities, likes, and dislikes.

The book provides a place to begin, avoiding errors and facilitating consistency of care from one setting to another. By providing information through pictures and descriptions, ideas and strategies that were successful or ineffective in the past do not go astray during the transition. In turn, potentially explosive situations or episodes of frustration for the individual and others decrease.

Additionally, a transitional photo book provides the individual with an identity of his or her own by illustrating personality and daily routines. At times, the transitional photo book gives a voice to those who cannot speak for themselves and provides others information to talk with them about. A photo book can teach a skill, enable the individual to review the skill, and help caretakers be more consistent with its implementation.

Fact Sheet

A fact sheet provides written information about diagnosis, specific strategies and adaptations, and general information about the individual. It enhances understanding and accurate interpretation of the person's behaviors and communication abilities. These informational tools are useful in the school setting, at home for relatives and sitters, and in the community at a work site. (See Appendix G.)

Information Poster

Strategically placed posters, frequently including both photos and written instructions, provide important information regarding care and interventions for a specific individual. Posters let staff members (even unfamiliar ones) view specific strategies and adaptations. For example, the poster could show equipment needs, feeding information, and positioning strategies. A poster may display the sequence and steps of an activity that can be used not only by the caretaker, but also by the individual to aid in completion of a task.

Daily Communication Log

This is a notebook therapists use for communication. Because a therapist may have a limited time to write, a preformatted checklist is ideal. The therapist can quickly fill out the checklist to provide information specific to the individual and important for the caretaker. Pamela's Day, on the next page, is an example of a simple communications log.

Digital Photos

Digital photos convey information about an individual. They are excellent visual prompts to assist in communication among the individual, the parent or caregiver, and professionals.

Pamela's Day

Date: _____

My health today was... _____

I ate a food that was not in my lunch: _____

Don't forget:
_____
_____

Things I need:
_____
_____

I really liked...
_____
_____
_____

Temper tantrums: _____

Why I was upset:
_____
_____

My disposition:
Cheerful
Attentive
Energetic
Tired
Did not listen
Did not participate

My behavior was...

Weekly "Homework Calendar"

A posted written or pictorial calendar with a list of homework tasks reinforces and generalizes learned skills. Homework should be functional and fun. A functional activity at home can be to practice categorizing and sorting. Examples: putting away the silverware, matching socks, or sorting white and colored clothes for the laundry.

Oral and Feeding Treatment

The primary objective of oral and feeding intervention for children is to resolve or decrease sensory difficulties and to create necessary adaptations. For the older population, even though we now believe that changes over time can occur, a greater emphasis on adaptations is appropriate.

General Recommendations

Develop a relationship and trust prior to intervening. Consider the parents, teachers, and paraprofessionals as the main interventionists, supported by specialists like a speech and occupational therapists. In addition:

- Use transition strategies like visuals and sensory calming activities to prepare for oral intervention or feeding.

- Introduce interventions slowly. Encourage, but do not force, participation in the activity.

- Use distractions like games and interests (music or a favorite toy, for example) to facilitate intervention.

- Be consistent in treatment.

- Communicate frequently with other team members. This is essential.

- Revisit issues periodically with the same or altered strategies because improvements may be gradual and slow.
- Be aware of how the environment affects the individual's level of arousal and make adjustments as appropriate.
- Be aware of food or latex allergies.
- Incorporate modeling by a peer or caretaker.

Proprioceptive/Tactile

- Encourage the child to mouth toys when it is age-appropriate.
- Introduce a toothbrush as early as possible.

- Provide vibration by using an electric toothbrush, which can be less annoying to the orally defensive individual.
- Apply pressure to cheeks, lips, and tongue prior to and during feeding (e.g., young children may enjoy a modified game of "peek a boo," where pressure is applied to their cheeks and lips using a soft cloth).
- Wipe face regularly with a warm cloth if tolerated, using pressure rather than a light touch.
- Use the Nuk Massage Brush® during the day, prior to and during feeding. Place food on the Nuk, put it in the child's mouth, and roll it—applying pressure between the gums and cheek. Roll it side to side on the tongue. The child's tolerance determines length of activity, so do not force.
- Allow children to chew on functional, age-appropriate edibles and non-edibles to assist with oral-seeking behaviors (e.g., sports cup with a straw, "boat" key chain, gum, gummi bears, licorice, pretzels, etc.). Crunchy, chewy foods promote oral strength.
- Consider creating an "oral box" (see Appendix F) or fanny pack filled with appropriate "chewies." This can help address pica, which is an abnormal craving to chew non-edibles like paint or dirt.
- Provide opportunities for blowing and sucking activities; e.g., whistles, harmonicas, blowing bubbles, blowing colored liquid through clear straws, drinking thickened liquid through straws (applesauce, Jell-O, etc.).
- Set appropriate sitting posture at mealtime: head upright and on midline, chin slightly tucked, back straight,

and feet supported. If needed, use boundaries in high chair or other seats.

Taste Suggestions

- Introduce the most similar tastes first.

- Add new tastes in minute doses to familiar or preferred tastes and increase as the individual begins to tolerate the new taste.

- Place a new taste on lips—allow for exploration.

- Introduce a new taste with pressure, (i.e., apply pressure to the tongue with a spoon).

- Give individuals control over the spoon, Nuk with food, etc. when appropriate.

- Provide well-seasoned and sweet-flavored foods.

Food Suggestions for Children and Adults

Arousing	**Calming**
Crunchy	Chewy
dried cereal	raisins
apples, raw vegetables	bagels
crackers, pretzels	fruity chews
popcorn	licorice
granola bars	
Spicy foods	Sweet foods
Cold foods	Warm foods
drinks, ice chips, Popsicles®	hot chocolate drinks
	oatmeal

Consider the following changes to compensate for sensory difficulties:

Nosey cup—A cutout in the rim of this cup allows for drinking without having to tilt one's head back. This may help an individual who has vestibular issues.

Sports cup—The benefits of a sports cup include holding and squeezing it as a fidget and sucking through or chewing on the straw to provide calming input during stressful times.

Large grip utensils, weighted utensils, scoop plates, plate guards, and Dycem® or other nonskid material under plates, are all adaptations that facilitate eating.

Chapter Eight

Developing Communication Skills

The following provides specific suggestions to facilitate increased communication according to the ability level of the individual. Each section includes a brief description of the individuals for whom the interventions are designed.

Individuals with Severe Difficulties

Individuals with severe difficulties communicating tend to avoid interaction, are upset by the proximity of others, do not request their needs, and have little or no functional speech or vocalizations.

Suggested Interventions

- Gradually engage the child in a motivating activity.
- Develop routines self-stimulatory or repetitive behaviors.
- Expand routines to increase the child's engagement; whenever possible, make it functional.
- Provide words to accompany actions and label objects, persons, and places as appropriate.
- Consider rough and tumble play may to facilitate engagement; especially with hard-to-engage children. However, this can be overwhelming for some. We do not recommend this strategy at bedtime.
- Interrupt or "sabotage" activity to reengage the child. This motivates the child to initiate communication.

- Teach basic action directives such as "Come here," "Stop," and "Sit down." The nature of these allows the interventionist to literally walk the individual through them. Consistent compliance with basic directives opens the door for further learning across all settings.

- Teach communication by using basics signs like "more."

- Use an exchange system like the Picture Exchange Communication System© (PECS) or natural gestures (pointing or turning palm upward to request). Start with words that are the most motivating.

- Re-enforce communication attempts to encourage practice as the individual experiences success. For example, a vocalization that gets a child a wanted ball eventually may result the child saying the word "ball."

- Provide choices to encourage initiation. For example, a choice between a ball or a puzzle may cause a child making a selection by looking, gesturing, vocalizing, or saying the word.

- Pair a motor movement to a sound or word that is motivating to the child. (Say, "Pop!" as a child is popping bubbles.)

- Encourage vocalizations through vestibular input and movement.

- Sing motivating familiar tunes and "sabotage" this activity by interrupting to encourage the child to sing along.

- Encourage imitative verbal behaviors during functional tasks that are motivating. For example, model the word "water" when the person wants a drink of water.

- Using "Motherese," an animated, intonation pattern frequently used to communicate with infants, can be attention-getting when working with this population.

- Teach protesting behavior by presenting tolerable aversive situations for practice. A placemat with the word "No" may be touched to refuse a presented food.

Early on, consider pairing verbal speech with an assistive or alternative system. This will not prevent verbal speech, and it may decrease frustration and behavioral problems. In addition, this sort of system provides a functional communication system if the child remains nonverbal.

Individuals with Moderate Difficulties

Individuals with moderate difficulties in communication tolerate others if encouraged and supported. They display emerging communication and initiate mostly for basic needs and physical stimulation. They may have echolalic speech and have "out-of-the-ordinary" interest in symmetry and collecting.

Suggested Interventions

- Increase periods of engagement by using child-directed/motivated activities that are adult-controlled. Controlling pieces or parts of toys (e.g., blocks or crayons) can be one way to prolong engagement. Use interest in symmetry and collecting to increase engagement. Slowly build tolerance for deviations in symmetry. Provide "sensory" breaks and discontinue the activity before an unworkable level of arousal is reached.

- Teach mechanisms to demonstrate protesting behavior. For example, teach the individual to use the word "move" when the proximity of others is no longer tolerated.

- Encourage communication for purposes other than accessing needs, such as to share information, "Look," or to greet, "Hi."

- Set up motivating situations to encourage meaningful use of echolalic speech. For example, pair repetitive counting with a functional task such as the number of times the child jumps on a trampoline.

- Use volume of speech to stimulate mitigated echolalia—the ability to extrapolate key words from a model. The interventionist models and emphasizes by using, in a slightly louder, volume the key words the child should use.

- Continue to functionally practice labels (names of things) and action words as they occur throughout the day.

- Initially, teach phrase production of two words by keeping one word constant; for example, "_Want_ cake," and "_Want_ water." Conversely, others may learn by using completely different phrases such as, "Ride bike," and "Want cookie."

- Provide opportunities to physically experience concepts such as near-far and front-back.

Individuals with Mild Difficulties

Individuals with mild difficulties in communication have sentence speech but have one-sided conversations, obsessions, and difficulties with social communication

Suggested Interventions

Social Stories

When describing a characteristic often seen in those with autism, Dr. Simon Baron-Cohen coined the phrase "mindblindness" to describe a person's inability to understand other people as having feelings, intentions, and views of the world other than their own. He also points out that often individuals with autism have a high propensity for rule-based systems. Carol Gray developed the concept of social stories, which help to compensate for mindblindness through carefully crafted, rule-based explanations.

Social stories provide information regarding situations and appropriate behavior. They can address pragmatics and social behavior issues. Carol Gray has written a series of social story books with numerous pre-written stories that address a variety of subjects and situations. These stories may be used independently or as an outline to develop a narrative to fit a specific need.

Depending on one's comprehension, a social story may be presented through pictures, pictures with words, or words alone. The interventionist should review new social stories with the individual and subsequently encourage reading the story more than once a day. Social stories provide opportunities for frequent review, thus enhancing one's skills.

The social world is very difficult for the individual with autism to comprehend. Social stories describe in concrete terms, situations, experiences, concepts, and rules of social behavior, using a written or pictorial format, facilitating better understanding of the social rules and nuances that others learn naturally. Stories should be written at the child's developmental level. For example, if he is a beginning reader, use pictures and words. Simple wording with emphasis on positive behavior rather than on negative behavior is essential.

Barrier Game

Use visuals to aid comprehension and expression. The barrier game is an excellent way to provide this. Provide identical items to the individual and instructor, starting with two-to-four items, depending on the level of development. Set up a barrier, such as a manila folder so that neither can see the other person's items.

The instructor then tells the individual what to do with his items (e.g., "Put the pencil into the cup."), while at the same time doing the task herself. After the individual shows that he has completed the task, the instructor lifts the barrier, producing a concrete visual of the correct answer.

Additional Interventions

- Teach ways to learn conversation turn-taking: when to start, when to stop, and how to switch topics. Use a prop, like a ball to provide a concrete visual for turn-taking.

- Make "figurine play scripts" with accompanied written activity.

- Use role-playing, which provides modeling to increase social communication skills. You can also use videos for this purpose.

Using Visuals to Communicate

A significant number of people with autism and related conditions demonstrate visual strengths, especially when compared to auditory abilities. Various visual methods can increase communication skills. Use visuals to:

- Enhance an individual's ability to learn to speak
- Help the individual to communicate using an assistive device
- Serve as an alternative system of communication

Visual information, in contrast to auditory information, is concrete and permanent. Once something is said, it is gone and cannot be retrieved unless someone repeats it. The permanency of a visual cue provides the opportunity for additional time to process information or have it available to revisit. An individual can use well-devised visuals to communicate with others. Over time, this can increase communication skills.

Visuals for communication can include objects, words, letters, or pictures. Objects may represent another object or concept. For instance, a cup can represent a cup or it can be a request for a drink. A toy cup can become the visual for the "real" cup. Pictures or words used in communication may include drawings, commercial icons, or photographs (digital cameras have made this medium very practical and easy to use).

The Picture Exchange Communication System by Frost/Bondy (PECS)

This is a popular and easy-to-use visual assistance system to facilitate communication. PECS gives nonverbal individuals the first step in the process of learning how to communicate. At times, a nonverbal child may be unaware that he has the ability to communicate his wants and needs. This program provides a step-by-step procedure and has a visual representation of what the child finds motivating. Once the child attempts to "go for" the motivating item, he receives the visual to offer in exchange for the item.

Initial physical prompting may be necessary. Decrease prompts as the child masters the skill and spontaneously requests an item or activity with the use of the visual. Introduce new visuals one at a time. Consistent use of this system helps master and maintain learned concepts.

As an aid to consistent use of PECS, attach pictures to a Velcro vest worn by the caretaker or put Velcro-backed pictures on strategically placed poster boards. For example, place food items in the kitchen (on the refrigerator, for example). If the child is interested in videos, strategically place pictures or the covers of favorite videos for him to use to request a specific video. Organize pictures by categories and place them in ziploc bags or containers. Ultimately, the child progresses from using single words, to phrases, to sentences.

Steps at a Glance

- Determine what items are important for the individual; e.g., music, food, etc. Use pictures or line drawings.

- Target one object. When the individual goes for the object, he receives the picture to offer in exchange for the object.

- Gradually remove physical prompting as the individual masters the skill and spontaneously makes requests with the use of the pictures.

- Introduce new pictures one at a time. Require the individual to keep skills by using pictures consistently.

- Facilitate picture exchange by placing them on a Velcro vest or poster.
- Organize pictures by categories and place them in ziploc bags, containers, etc.

Communication Boards

Communication boards, some of which provide voice output, provide low-tech to very sophisticated ways in which to encourage speech production or support an alternative means of communicating. Symbols on communication boards may vary from letters to spell words, basic words, pictures or photos, line drawings, to commercially available computer programs.

From time to time, parents and professionals have concerns regarding the use of augmentative or alternative systems to communicate. The concern is that a child may become dependent on the alternative system, stifling his potential for verbal communication. The literature has discarded this argument and, in fact, the opposite is the case. Visual systems increase a child's potential for speech production.

Visual or Photo Books

Visual or photo books are fabricated booklets designed to increase communication skills. These include pictures and names of items and are used to increase vocabulary through labeling. For example, a visual book might include a photograph or line drawing of a table, with the word "table" adjacent to the picture.

The interventionist can make photo books by filling several pages of a small photograph album with pictures that an individual can use to indicate needs and wants. Begin with one picture per page. As attention span and language improves, increase the number of pages and pictures per page. Have the individual turn pages to find certain pictures and name or point to them. This is a motivating way for children to work on expressive and receptive vocabulary.

Benefits:

- Labels and identifies items (e.g. favorite CDs or videos)
- Identifies family, peers, and friends
- Labels actions (e.g., run, or jump)
- Facilitates responses to questions of "what, where, when, who, and how?"

- Increases verbal interaction
- Suggests conversation topics
- Provides a precursor to using an alternative system of communication (if needed)

Experiential or Communication Stories

These describe events through the use of pictures, photos, drawings, or words for the purpose of language development. Pairing language with an experience enhances understanding of the event or activity and provides more opportunities to practice language. For example, when asking a child, "What did you do today?" the interventionist may draw pictures and provide words to describe the child eating, playing, etc. Using experiential and communication stories develops language skills—progressing from simple to complex development.

Chapter Nine[1]
Using Videos

When working with the multifaceted difficulties that can affect individuals with autism and related sensory integration disorders, an intensive therapeutic team approach is the most effective. Parents are integral members of their child's treatment team. Their daily experiences result in some of the most innovative and beneficial techniques and strategies to facilitate learning. As professionals interact with parents, they learn new strategies that they can apply to situations with a variety of children. One powerful, parent-inspired technique is the use of videos.

> *Tammy G. used a video for teaching her four-year-old daughter Pamela, a child diagnosed with autism, because Pamela did not appear curious or interested in her newborn brother David. In fact, she purposefully avoided contact with him. However, she was very interested in videos— especially those that included cartoon characters and music. For this reason, Tammy decided to "introduce" David to Pamela through this medium. The video was a brief segment showing David lying in his crib with Tammy narrating what David was doing. Pamela's favorite toy was attached to David's crib during the videotaping to further encourage her interest. Since Pamela enjoyed bath time, David was also videotaped in the tub. Shortly thereafter, Pamela developed an interest in her brother. This let their relationship develop.*

---

[1] Part of this chapter is reprinted with permission from the article: Kashman, Nancy, et al. "Using Videotapes to Help Children with Autism." *OT Practice.* July 3, 2000. ©American Occupational Therapy Association, Inc.

The literature suggests that videos allow children with autism to learn in a medium that is more appropriate to their learning styles. A significant number of them are visual learners (Grandin, 1995). Frequently, children with autism have difficulties with eye contact and gaze, which are arousing (Miller, 1996). Using videos to teach a skill to children with autism can eliminate that added stress. Charlop and Milstein's study (1989) found that using videos was not only effective in increasing social communications skills in children with autism but also helped the children maintain and generalize the skills learned. Videos are predictable, can be tailored to specific interests, and allow multiple viewings. Videos let children with autism work through some of their difficulties and phobias.

Luscre and Center's study (1996) used video training to reduce "dental phobia" in children with autism. They used three basic techniques. They provided calming toys/activities throughout the exam, video viewing followed by practice of the procedure in a simulated setting, and the child's favorite reinforcers/rewards. Results were very favorable. Children with autism exhibit "tunnel vision" (Lovaas, Schreibman, Koegel, Rhem, 1971), which is the ability to focus on one stimulus or part of a "whole." Set in an optimal environment, videos offer learning tailored to fit the individual's needs.

In our practice, we use videos for a variety of reasons, from assessment to intervention. Used as an adjunct to an evaluation, videos offer the opportunity to more accurately assess a child's skill level by observing the child within his natural environment without the impact of the examiner.

Assessed skills assessed may include social, communication, motor, cognitive/academic, and self-help.

Children with autism exhibit sensory processing difficulties that are frequently difficult to assess in a clinical setting. During the natural course of a day, videos can provide insight into a child's ability to process sensory information. A child's reactions to the world around him, his level of arousal, and any avoiding or seeking behaviors may appear. The team can assess his play skills, need for personal space, sociability, and response to touch.

Gross and fine motor skills, such as general posture, balance, and fluidity of movement; manipulation; spatial perception; and motor planning skills are seen as the individual navigates his environment. Additionally, videos provide an effective means of documenting progress over time. The observer can note the child's attention span and stamina by the length of time the individual remains on a task and his ability to transition and shift his attention. Videos often provide us with a view of the antecedents when self-injurious behaviors/stereotypic behaviors are an issue.

Observation of the environment is necessary for future intervention. Modifying the environment is often the easiest and quickest way to facilitate change. As the effect of the environment builds over time, simple changes can help maintain a child's appropriate level of arousal needed for intervention.

Things to look at in the environment include the noise level and the child's reaction to it. Visual stimuli, which include wall decor and clutter, can easily be modified if the child appears to react to it. When looking at toys or equipment, note if there are special toys he seeks or avoids. Additionally, viewing others in the child's environment, their interaction, and the child's response, provides information to the caretakers and allows ongoing intervention. As interventionists, we can assess our own interactions and capture reactions and behaviors that we may miss when we are in the middle of a session.

Videos also facilitate the development of goals and objectives. Intervention videos can enhance individuals' ability to learn about themselves and the world around them. Videos may be commercial videos or child-specific.

Homemade, child-specific, intervention videos facilitate the development of a variety of skills, provide "drills" during extended school breaks to avoid regression of achieved skills, and prepare the child for transitions. The older individual may benefit from videos for prevocational or vocational training and social skills. See the guidelines for suggestions on producing child-specific videos.

Guidelines for the Production of Intervention Videos

- Develop videos by a thorough analysis of an individual's needs and interests. We recommend a task analysis of the targeted skill.
- Prepare a script prior to taping. For prepared scripts, Carol Gray's *Social Stories* is helpful.
- Imbed challenging activities into familiar and interesting tasks, such as handwriting and bathing.

- Be aware of an individual's attention span. Try to expand the attention span by including "grabbers" like music and movement.

- Speak clearly and eliminate nonessential speech. Allow time for responses between activities.

- Repeat activities more than once, if necessary.

- Simplify video scenes by filtering out extraneous objects, sounds, and movements that can clutter and confuse the individual.

- Isolate the skill you want to develop and provide prompts. Label objects, persons, and actions as appropriate.

- Provide a variety of examples to help the learner to generalize the lesson.

- Keep manipulatives and objects used in the video handy so that the individual can use them while watching the video.

- Interaction or practice with an instructor or peer during, in between, or after the video, can increase learning.

- Reintroduce all forms of stimulation, because some people are not interested in videos. The individual may develop an interest over time. Never force; just encourage.

- Introduce "real people" slowly—many children will initially only watch cartoon videos. Peers and familiar persons or objects can be especially interesting.

- Do not overuse the video to the point of boredom.

- Obtain prior consent of parent or caregiver to resolve confidentiality issues.

Chapter 10
Teaming Case Studies

Taking an OT and SLP team approach to implementing sensory and communication strategies requires close coordination, mutual respect, and a willingness to improvise. The following case studies illustrate how the benefits of a team approach reinforce and enhance the knowledge, skills, and abilities of the team members, providing better and more effective treatment. The team's ability to improvise proved particularly important. Because of the location—El Salvador—the team did not have access to a wide range of therapy supplies and equipment.

Training

Those involved had not worked together previously, and working effectively as members of a team requires training and practice. The first step was to orient the team members who would evaluate and treat affected children. An introductory seminar for approximately eighty therapists, teachers, parents, and administrators included an overview of sensory integration and communication difficulties, functional intervention, and teaming to provide a comprehensive intervention plan for the home and classroom.

Teaming, at first glance, may appear to be a simple concept and an easy skill to develop. The concept of teaming is not new, but it is often difficult to implement. Experience has demonstrated that effective teaming is an ongoing and always evolving process. When teaming, the development of new techniques and strategies are continuous as one learns from the child, the family, caretakers, and other interventionists. The result of working together is synergistic, as several "heads and hands together" often elicit more creative interventions.

Lack of teaming hinders communication and may result in treating a child segmentally rather than holistically. For example, a parent reported that several interventionists worked with her child but had never communicated with each other. As a result of the seminar in El Salvador, everyone had a better understanding of how to work as members of a team. Subsequently, the group re-formed into small teams for problem solving, strategizing, and treatment.

Christina

A team approach was evident when treating Christina, a 3-year-old girl diagnosed with a rare genetic disorder called trisomy eight. She was receiving physical therapy, and her mother wanted additional functional strategies to embed in Christina's day. A brief assessment included parental questioning and "play" with Christina by a team that included a special education teacher, an OT, and an SLP. The child's mother, sister, and nanny also participated, providing observations of Christina's behavior since birth.

Christina, a charming and personable child, presented overall hypotonicity with decreased strength and endurance. These difficulties impacted her general posture, movements, and communication. Although Christina's speech articulation was clear, verbalizing was an effort. Her low volume and brief, infrequently produced phrases hindered her communication. Christina's sitting balance was unstable. Her low tone caused her to "crash" into those supporting her. To provide support for sitting, the use of "stuffed pants" was considered to provide boundaries and postural support.

After an exchange of ideas and information, the team suggested:

- Use music to motivate Christina to increase vocalization, vocabulary, and participation in motor tasks
- Place many of her toys on a vertical plane slightly at or above eye level to facilitate trunk extension, develop upper body strength, and increase voice volume
- Encourage Christina to play in a variety of tactile substances such as dry beans, rice, or sand to provide hand-strengthening games and to give her an increased opportunity to investigate new textures
- Use alternative seating, such as stuffed pants, to provide additional postural support

The Orphanage

The team visited an orphanage for children with special needs. The residents' ages ranged from birth to adult. The orphanage did not have any occupational or speech language therapists, but did have physical therapists, who were quite adept at fabricating seating adaptations. They used readily available but low cost materials, like Styrofoam and cardboard boxes. The visiting occupational therapist teamed with the physical therapists to develop appropriate strategies and identify needed interventions. Together, they developed functional requirements for a dynamic thumb abductor splint for one of the children. The speech therapist shared with the staff therapists simple but effective communication strategies, such as providing more time for a child with autism to respond.

Anna

With her permission, the team made a video of Anna, a bright, articulate, thirty-eight-year-old woman who were severely affected by juvenile arthritis. Amazingly, although her fingers are severely contracted, Anna had sufficient grasp to create beautiful, woven, infant headbands. Due to her dependency in the area of self-help, the therapists requested exploring adaptations to facilitate independence in feeding. Making a video enabled the team members to consult with specialists who were not able to travel to the remote location. This enabled the team to provide Anna with adaptive equipment. She is now able to feed herself.

Conclusions

As a result of their experience with a teaming approach to sensory and communication strategies, the authors have concluded that therapists are most effective when they work in teams, and teams are most effective when the members are creative, take risks, and learn from each other.

Appendices

Appendix A
Sensory Integration Disorders

Dysfunction in sensory integration affects a wide variety of people, including a significant percentage who are also affected by other developmental conditions. Those other conditions sometimes exacerbate or mask sensory issues. Therapists should therefore be alert to the possibility of co-existing conditions when assessing and treating people with sensory dysfunctions. This appendix briefly describes a number of developmental conditions that may coexist with dysfunction in sensory integration.

The Autism Spectrum

Autism is one of several disorders that falls under the umbrella of pervasive developmental disorder (PDD). These are generally recognized as involving three impairments: language and communication, social interaction, and imaginative play—including restricted interests and activities.

While physicians look for these three hallmarks to diagnosis of autism, there are other symptoms that are common, but by no means universal: odd, or repetitive behaviors; lack of eye contact; impaired gait and posture; sensory difficulties; and problems with attention/motivation. As our knowledge and understanding of individuals with autism has increased, we realize that an increasing number of individuals go through life experiencing difficulties with sensory integration. In most cases, these sensory difficulties interfere with the person's ability to interact with (and make sense of) his world.

Autism is a lifelong disability that typically appears during the first three years of a child's life. We now call autism a spectrum disorder (ASD)—the symptoms and behaviors can present themselves in a wide variety of combinations, ranging from mild to severe. Severe behaviors can include self-injury. In addition to autism, many other diagnoses involve sensory integration difficulties.

Asperger's Syndrome

Asperger's Syndrome includes individuals who typically do not present with delays in language acquisition or cognitive development. However, they do exhibit difficulties with social behaviors and have tendencies toward obsessive interests.

Pervasive Developmental Disorder Not Otherwise Specified (PDD/NOS)

Individuals exhibit many of the symptoms of autism, but not all. The symptoms may be less severe than those of autism, but they do not meet the criteria for the diagnosis of other disorders, such as mental retardation or attention deficit hyperactivity disorder.

Childhood Disintegrative Disorder

This is a rare variation of PDD. A marked loss of skills in communication, social, and self-help skills, and, sometimes, motor skills, follows a period of at least two years of normal development. This primarily affects boys.

Rett Syndrome

This syndrome is a movement disorder characterized by stereotypic hand wringing and mental retardation. It presents itself following a six-to-eighteen month period of normal development. Associated deficits include loss of language and motor skills and self-injurious behavior. Rett Syndrome generally occurs only females. A regression in cognition and behavior, social, and motor skills is noted throughout the lifetime of those affected.

Disorders with Autistic Features

Landau-Kleffner Syndrome

This syndrome causes a rapid loss of language between three- and seven-years-of-age, with clinical seizures in up to eighty percent of cases. These seizures have a direct impact on language loss. The individuals first lose their ability to comprehend (i.e., receptive speech) and then their ability to speak (i.e., expressive speech), with changes occurring gradually or suddenly. Characteristics include failure to respond to sounds, pain insensitivity, aggression, poor eye contact, insistence on sameness, and sleep problems. It is twice as common in males as in females.

Fragile X

Individuals with this disorder often present with repetitive motor behaviors, hypersensitivity to sound, hyposensitivity or hypersensitivity to oral or facial stimulation, and mild-to-severe cognitive delays.

Neurofibromatosis

This hereditary disorder involves the development of tumors of the peripheral nerves. Location of the tumors can affect neuromotor, sensory, and/or intellectual functioning.

Tuberous Sclerosis

This is a congenital disease characterized by tumors of the lateral ventricle and sclerotic patches on the brain. Progressive cognitive dysfunction and seizures occur.

Prader-Willi Syndrome

This syndrome has features that include obsession with food and impulsive eating. Delays in language and motor development occur. Characteristics also include infant feeding problems, sleep disturbances, skin picking, temper tantrums, tactile hyposensitivity, and poor muscle tone. Most individuals with this syndrome have cognitive impairment.

Williams Syndrome

This is a genetic disorder characterized by mild mental retardation and unique, pixie-like, facial features. Behaviors include developmental and language delays, difficulties with gross motor skills, hypersensitivity to sounds, picky eating, and perseveration. This population is very sociable.

Hyperlexia

This disorder includes an intense fascination with letters, numbers, patterns, and logos. The individuals have a self-taught precocious ability to read (not necessarily with comprehension), spell, write, or compute, usually before the age of five. The individuals have difficulty developing language and communication skills. They often exhibit unusual behaviors or interests. There is less effect on social interactions than experienced with autism.

Conditions With Sensory Integration Difficulties

The criteria for diagnosis of the following impairments do not necessarily include difficulties with sensory integration. However, neuromuscular limitations, developmental delays, or medical issues can cause either primary or secondary sensory integration impairments to occur.

Cerebral Palsy

Professionals often describe cerebral palsy as a sensory-motor disorder. Usually, most of the emphasis in treatment is directed toward the motor and movement difficulties. Frequently, individuals with cerebral palsy exhibit problems with sensory integration that are primary or secondary in nature. The primary deficits are those that occur concurrently with the movement disorder. Secondary deficits are those that are the result of the movement disorder.

Down Syndrome

This is the most common chromosomal abnormality. Most areas of development are affected to a lesser or greater degree, including cognition, motor skills, communication, and sensory skills.

Others

Prematurity, attention deficit disorders, behavior disorders, learning disabilities, Alzheimer's disease, chronic illness, fetal alcohol syndrome, and traumatic brain injury can cause difficulties in processing sensory information from the environment and one's body. This can cause difficulties in attention, behavior, learning, speech development, and movement patterns. At times, the symptoms we see with the individuals suffering from one of these disorders are due to sensory integration problems.

Appendix B
Guide to Assessment of Environment

The following is an informal guide that the authors developed to assess a classroom environment. You may modify this and use it for home and work settings.

Name _____

Date _____

Area _____

Examiner _____

Directions: Investigate the various sensory experiences of your classroom. Observations should be the result of naturally occurring events: physical surroundings as well as other individuals in the environment. Environmental modifications should be reasonable and practical. Some examples are provided for clarity.

                                          Observation   Needs

I. Room Organization
  A. Overall safety of room
  B. Ease of movement around area
  C. Orderliness and efficiency of room (clutter, everything in its place)
  D. Existing modifications
  E. Individual reactions

II. Noise Level
  A. Overall noise level
  B. Unexpected noises
    1. Cause (phone, bell, etc.)
    2. Frequency
    3. Duration
    4. Intensity (how loud)

Observation Needs

    C. Existing modifications
    D. Individual reaction
        1. Immediate
        2. Delayed (i.e., escalates)
        3. Degree (mild, moderate, or severe)

III. Visual Stimuli
    A. Type of visual stimuli
        1. Static or moving
        2. Patterns or colors
    B. Quantity of visual stimuli
    C. Lighting (shadows, fluorescent, or natural)
    D Existing modifications
    E. Individual reaction
        1. Immediate
        2. Delayed (i.e., escalates)
        3. Degree (mild, moderate, or severe)

IV. Odors
    A. List any noticable odors
       (from meals, cooking, art activities, etc.)
    B. Existing modifications
    C. Individual reaction
        1. Immediate or delayed (i.e., escalates)
        2. Degree (mild, moderate, or severe)

V. Temperature
    A. Temperature of area
    B. Changes in temperature
    C. Existing modifications
    D. Individual reaction
        1. Immediate
        2. Delayed (i.e., escalates)
        3. Degree (mild, moderate, or severe)

                                                    Observation   Needs

VI. Available Equipment (Tactile, Proprioceptive, and Vestibular)
  A. Gross motor (swings, exercise equipment)
  B. Seating (gliders, rocking chair, beanbag chair)
  C. How is this equipment used?
  D. Modifications implemented
  E. Individual reaction

VI. Environmental Visual Supports
  A. Describe current visual supports available
  B. Describe individual reactions

VII. Others in the environment (e.g., caretakers, parents, teachers, and peers)
  A. Describe current visual supports available
  B. Describe individual reactions

Stuffed Pants

Appendix C
Stuffed Pants

It is often quite difficult to appropriately position the severely challenged individual. Although there are fine pieces of equipment that you can purchase, they are often quite expensive and, at times, bulky and large. Using cushions or pillows can sometimes provide support. However, these frequently slip and often do not provide adequate support. Use stuffed pants for positioning a severely challenged individual in supine, side lying, prone, or unsupported sitting. Individuals with sensory processing difficulties often seek increased proprioceptive input. A beanbag chair or "stuffed pants" can provide this input.

Stuffed pants are quick, inexpensive pieces of equipment that serve many purposes. These pants are easily made from sweatpants or other soft material and are stuffed with foam or other malleable material. Securely close the legs and waist of the pants with large rubber bands. Not closing them permanently allows washing and appropriate sanitary care. When providing these pants to individuals who mouth objects, use caution.

Stuffed Sweatshirt

Sew closed

Sew closed

Appendix D
Stuffed Sweatshirt

Tactile exploration is a critical part of normal development. Most preschool and kindergarten classes have "tables" filled with water, sand, dried beans, and rice. Some of our students are unable to participate in this type of play due to mouthing. Using stuffed sweatshirts prevents students from mouthing while they manipulate small objects. It encourages tactile exploration and the development of discrimination skills. Additionally, placed on one's lap, this tool provides proprioceptive input. Encourage exploration and hide small objects to increase interest and develop language. Incorporate vocabulary and labeling of objects.

The stuffed sweatshirt is easy to make. Sew the neck and waist of a sweatshirt. Fill the shirt through the sleeves with dried beans, rice, or noodles. The student can explore the contents by placing hands and arms into the sleeves (assistance may be needed for placement). Consider the size of the shirt in relation to the size of the student. We recommend supervision during this activity. When the shirt is not in use, fastening rubberbands around the cuffs will prevent spilling the contents.

Weighted Vest

Cut off sleeves and make four pockets to fill with weights

Sew two "pockets" on front of vest and two "pockets on back. Close with Velcro® or basted stitch.

Appendix E
Weighted Vests

Consult with a trained therapist when considering adding weighted materials.

Using weighted garments provides proprioceptive input and often can reduce an individual's level of arousal during demanding times (such as transition and seatwork).

Weighted Vests

- Not recommended for individuals who have respiratory difficulties, asthma, or who are pregnant.

- Twenty-to-thirty minutes on, and at least one hour off.

- Individualize weight to each person. Start with small amounts of evenly distributed weight and add or reduce weight as appropriate.

- Size is not always an indication of weight needs. Vest manufacturers appear to recommend up to approximately 5% of the individual's weight. Adding more than 10% of a person's body weight is cause for orthopedic concern.

- Drooping shoulders, difficulty in moving, excessive mellowness, and lethargy are all symptoms of possible difficulty.

Fabricate vests from hunting, fishing, or fashion vests. Add "pockets" (two on front and two on back) for weights. You can cut sleeves off a zippered sweatshirt, using the material to fabricate pockets for the weights. However, this may not be suitable for heavier weights, due to stretching. Weights can be dried beans, washers, or fishing weights placed in small, sealed plastic bags or sewn fabric bags. Distribute the weights evenly. Position the pockets for weights so that they do not rest on the hips or legs when the individual is seated.

Use weighted vests with caution for individuals who may remove or mouth small objects.

Appendix F
Oral Box

The two types of oral sensory dysfunction, "hyper" (over-registration/defensive) and "hypo" (under-registration), result in mild-to-severe oral or feeding difficulties. Using an "oral box" can provide supplies at a therapist's fingertips and yet meet the child's specific needs.

An oral box provides individuals with edibles and non-edibles to assist with oral-seeking behaviors and can decrease a person's level of arousal.

You can fill the oral box with some of the following items: gum, gummy bears, Tootsie Rolls,® suckers, rocket suckers (promote lip rounding), squeeze pop (can place gel in specific spots), licorice, pretzels, graham crackers, edible bubbles, crunchy, chewy foods (promote oral strength), glycerin swabs, Nuk, whistles, bubbles, pacifiers, and various straws.

You can create a therapeutic oral box from a fisherman's tackle box. Large, two-level tackle boxes are especially useful. A number of items can be stored in the lower level of the box, and items specific for the individual being treated can be placed on the upper level. Very small tackle boxes can be specific for an individual and used as needed or recommended throughout the day.

Food Suggestions for Children and Adults

Arousing

Crunchy
- dried cereal
- apples, raw vegetables
- crackers, pretzels
- popcorn
- granola bars

Spicy foods

Cold temperature
- drinks, ice chips, Popsicles®

Calming

Chewy
- raisins
- bagels
- fruity chews
- licorice

Sweet foods

Warm temperature
- hot chocolate drinks

Appendix G
Example of a Fact Sheet

Pamela's Strengths and Challenges

General Information

Pamela turns nine in March. In reading, she has almost completed first grade, and in math, she is 80% complete in her kindergarten curriculum. Her overall knowledge is strong is some areas and weak in others. Do not underestimate her knowledge based on what she says. We have found she knows a lot more than we realize! Pamela does not seek to make friends, but she does not avoid children. Many autistic adults report years later that they wanted to make friends but had no idea how to do it or how to fit in with other children.

Pamela's Strengths

Pamela has an excellent visual memory—a skill that helped her to learn how to read. Her ability to read has allowed her to learn language and math more easily. Pamela possesses excellent computer skill, and she can learn from computer software. Pamela enjoys art activities and writing. She recently became interested in drawing pictures. Pamela can state her needs and ask simple questions. She also likes describing what she's doing when she is playing. Pamela is very observant and is very aware of events around her. She loves to do many activities in her free time that are beyond watching videos. Her activities include play, imagination, and reading.

Pamela's Challenges

Pamela has a hard time listening and remembering what she hears—this makes it difficult for her to learn language. She has not learned to hold a conversation. She is also hypersensitive to some sounds like fluorescent lights and elevators. Pamela is terrified of the sound elevators make. Some of her sound-hypersensitivity causes her to cry and tantrum.

Tips for Interacting with Pamela

Talking

Talk directly to Pamela and, if necessary, get down to her physical level and get closer to her. Make eye contact to get her attention, but don't require it all the time (some autistic people can use either or hearing, not both). Make short, simple statements with positive wording (tell her what to do rather than "stop it"). Avoid double meanings, jokes, sarcasm, etc.; because autistic people tend to take these literally. Allow her time to process what you asked and process her response (counting to five helps). Provide her with visual cues like gestures, writing, or drawing.

Behavior

When it comes to autism, view behavior (even negative) as a form of communication. My goal is to teach Pamela to use positive behaviors to obtain her needs. Imagine yourself in a situation where you were surrounded by loud noises and chaos. Then imagine that you are unable to speak. How are you going to let the world know that you are overwhelmed? Imagine yourself in situations where you are bored, frustrated, or just do not feel like doing anything, but do not know how to express your feelings. When you see

Pamela start to tantrum, this is what she is probably experiencing! Rather than viewing a tantrum as bratty behavior, ask yourself what is Pamela trying to say.

Look at Her Strengths

Pamela is very knowledgeable about many subjects. She will not be able to give long, detailed information, but she can answer simple questions. When asking questions, be specific (e.g., "What month?" is better than "When?"). When asking a yes/no question, cue her that it is a question: "Was George Washington born in December? Yes or no.") Let her show her thoughts by drawing pictures. Pamela loves talking about calendars, seasons, weather, animals, drawing, etc. She also loves questions in the form of a riddle: "I was born in February. My picture is on a quarter. I cut down a cherry tree when I was a boy. Who am I?"

Appendix H
General Communication Tips

For students with sensory integration difficulties, the world can be difficult to understand, with the most complex factor in the environment being "people." People are often unpredictable, loud, move too much, and touch too much. Using the following "tips" can enhance communication, decrease stress level, and improve overall function.

- Do not assume receptive language is adequate.
- Provide information in brief, clear, positive statements. Tell the student what you want him to do rather than what you do not want him to do.
- Use visuals when possible.
- Use sign language or universal signs to facilitate better comprehension.
- Lower speech volume when speaking.
- Prepare the student by communicating what you are about to do and provide information as you interact. This not only maintains calmness but also "teaches" language.
- Provide time for response.
- Use a "singsong" voice or exaggerated inflection to gain a person's attention.
- Remember that echolalic speech or "repeated speech" may convey meaning.

- Expand communication expressions; for example, if a child names the object "ball" you may add, "Let's play ball."
- Do not engage in excessive "talk" when a student is upset.
- Avoid sarcasm, innuendos, double meanings, and unclear statements.
- There are times when less information is better; if the child is mono-channel, decrease communication while he is engaged in a challenging task.
- Interact and relate every time you work with a student.

Appendix I
References

Assessment Sources

The Peabody Picture Vocabulary Test-Third Edition. Dunn, L.M., Dunn, L; American Guidance Service, Circle Pines, MN.

The Expressive One-Word Picture Vocabulary Test-2000 Edition, Brownell, Rick (editor); Psychological and Educational Publications, Inc, Hydesville, CA.

Preschool Language Scale-3 (PLS-3), Zimmerman, IL; Psychological Corp., San Antonio.

The Receptive/Expressive/Emergent Language Scale Revised-2 (REEL-2), Psychological and Educational Publications, Inc, Hydesville, CA.

The Sequential Inventory of Communication Development-Revised (SICD-R), Hedrick, DL, Prather, EM, Tobin, AR; Pro-Ed, Austin.

The Hawaii Early Learning Profile (HELP), Park, Stephanie; Therapro, Inc., Framingham, MA.

The Sensory Profile. Dunn, Winnie; Therapy Skill Builders, Division of Psychological Corporation, San Antonio.

The Sensory Integration Inventory-Revised for Individuals with Developmental Disabilities.

(SII-R), Hanschu, Bonnie, Reisman, Judith; PDP Press, Hugo, MN.

Peabody Developmental Motor Scale-2nd Edition, Folio, M. Rhonda, Fewell, Rebecca; Pro-Ed, Austin.

The Early Intervention Developmental Profile (EIDP)-Revised, Schafer, D. Sue, Morwich, Martha S. (editors); The University of Michigan Press, Ann Arbor.

The Preschool Developmental Profile (PDP), D'Eugenio, Diane, Moersch, Martha (editors); The University of Michigan Press, Ann Arbor.

The Beery Developmental Test of Visual Motor Integration (VMI), Beery, Keith, E., Buktenica, Norman; Pro-Ed, Austin.

The School Function Assessment (SFA), Coster, Wendy, et.al., Psychological Corporation/Therapy Skill Builders, San Antonio.

Recommended Readings

Anderson, Johanna M. *Sensory Motor Issues in Autism*. San Antonio: Therapy Skill Builders, 1999.

Attwood, Tony, and Temple Grandin. "Tony and Temple – Face-to-Face." *Autism/Asperger's Digest*. Jan-Feb. 2000.

Attwood, Tony. A*sperger's Syndrome: A Guide for Parents and Professionals*. (videotape). Arlington, TX: Future Horizons Inc., 1999.

— A*sperger's Syndrome: A Guide for Parents and Professionals*. London: Jessica Kingsley, 1998.

— "The Early Diagnosis of Autism." *The Morning News*. Spring 1997.

— Asperger's Syndrome

Ayres, A.J. *Sensory Integration and the Child*. Los Angeles: Western Psychological, 1979.

Baker, G, and K. Gester. "Vestibular Stimulation with Autistic and Schizophrenic Children." *Alabama Journal of Medical Sciences* 14 (1977): 434-35.

Ball, Donna. "Visual Supports: Helping Children With Autism." *OT Practice*. October 1999.

Bauer, B.A. "Sensory Reinforcement with Autistic Children." *Behavioral Psychotherapy* 13 (1977).

Baron-Cohen, S. *Mindblindness: An Essay on Theory Of Mind*. Boston: Massachusetts Institute of Technology, 1997.

Benbow, Mary, et al. *Handwriting in the Classroom; Classroom Applications for School-Based Practice*. Rockville, MD: AOTA, 1995.

Beversdorf, David Q, et al. "Brief Report: Macrographia in High-Functioning Adults with Autism Spectrum Disorder." *Journal of Autism and Developmental Disorders* 31/1 (2001).

Bissell, Julie, and Jessica Peng, Shu-Chin. "Assistive Technology to Support Sensory Integration, Praxis and Self-Regulation: Needs of Children with Autism." *Sensory Integration Special Interest Section Quarterly* 24/3 (2001).

Bissell, Julie, et al. *Sensory Motor Handbook: A Guide for Implementing and Modifying Activities in the Classroom.* Torrance, CA: Sensory Integration International

Blanche, Erna, et al. *Combining Neuro-Developmental Treatment and Sensory Integration Principles.* Tucson: Therapy Skill Builders, 1995.

Bright, T., and K. Bittick. "Reduction of Self-Injurious Behavior Using Sensory Integrative Techniques." *American Journal of Occupational Therapy* 35 (1981): 167-72.

Butrick-Wenger, Dorothy. "Using SI Techniques With Adults With Head Injury." *OT Practice.* November 1998.

Case-Smith, Jane. "Clinical Interpretation of 'Factor Analysis on the Sensory Profile from a National Sample of Children Without Disabilities.'" *American Journal of Occupational Therapy* 51/7 (1997): 496-499.

— *Pediatric Occupational Therapy and Early Intervention.* Newton, MA: Butterworth-Heinemann, 1993.

Charlop, M.H., and J.P. Milstein. "Teaching Autistic Children Conversational Speech Using Video Modeling." *Journal of Applied Behavioral Analysis* 22 (1989): 275-285.

Coleman, R.S., et al. "The Effects of Florescent and Incandescent Illumination upon Repetitive Behaviors in Autistic Children." *Journal of Autism and Developmental Disorders* 6 (1976)157-62.

Coling, Marcia Cain. *Developing Integrated Programs: A Transdisciplinary Approach for Early Intervention.* Tucson: Therapy Skill Builders, 1995.

Courchesne, E, et al. "Parietal Damage and Narrow 'Spotlight' Spatial Attention." *Journal of Cognitive Neuroscience* (January 1994).

Daw, Jennifer Cantello. "A Blueprint for Learning!" *Autism/Asperger's Digest* (May-June 2001).

Dellacecca, Patricia, et.al. "Creating Communication Boards and Displays." *Closing the Gap* 15/6 (1997).

Durand, V.M. "Motivation Assessment Scale." *Dictionary of Behavioral Assessment Techniques.* M. Hewsen and A.S. Bellack. New York: Pergamon, 1988.

Ermer, Julie, and Winnie Dunn. "The Sensory Profile: A Discriminate Analysis of Children with and without Disabilities." *American Journal of Occupational Therapy* 52/4 (1998): 283-289.

Favell, J.E., and J.F. McGimsey. "Treatment of Self-Injury by Providing Alternate Sensory Activities." *Analysis and Intervention in Developmental Disabilities* 2 (1982): 83-104.

Feldman, Jean. *Transition Time*. Beltsville: Grypon House, 1995.

Filipek, Pauline A., et al. "The Screening and Diagnosis of Autistic Spectrum Disorders." *Journal of Autism and Developmental Disorders* 28/6 (1999).

Fink, Barbara. *Sensory Motor Integration Activities*. Tucson: Therapy Skill Builders, 1993.

Fouse, Beth. *Creating a Win-Win IEP for Students with Autism*. Arlington, TX: Future Horizons, Inc., 1996.

Fouse, Beth, and Maria Wheeler. *A Treasure Chest of Behavioral Strategies*. Arlington, TX: Future Horizons,Inc., 1997.

Freeman, Sabrina, and Lorelei Dake. *Teach Me Language*. Langley: SKF, 1996.

Frost, Lori, and Andrew Bondy. *The Picture Exchange Communication System*. Cherry Hill: Pyramid Educational Consultants.

Gilliam, James . *Gilliam Autism Rating Scale*. Austin: Pro-Ed, 1995.

Grandin, Temple. *Emergence: Labeled Autistic*. Novato: Arena Press, 1986.

— *Sensory Challenges & Answers* (videotape). Arlington, TX: Future Horizons, Inc., 1998.

— *Thinking in Pictures*. New York: Doubleday, 1995.

Gray, Carol. *Comic Strip Conversations*. Arlington, TX: Future Horizons, Inc., 1994

— *The New Social Story Book: Illustrated Edition*. Arlington, TX: Future Horizons, Inc., 1994.

Greenspan, Stanley, and Serena Wieder. *The Child with Special Needs*. Reading, PA: Addison-Wesley, 1998.

Haack, Laurel, and Mary Haldy. "Making It Easy: Adapting Home and School Environments." *OT Practice* (November 1996).

Held, R., and A. Hein. "Movement -Produced Stimulation in the Development of Visually Guided Behavior." *Journal of Comparative and Physiological Psychology* 56/5.

Henderson, Anne, and Charlane Pehoski. *Hand Function in the Child*. St. Louis: Mosby Press, 1995.

Hanschu, Bonnie, and Judith Reisman. *Sensory Integration Inventory-Revised for Individuals with Developmental Disabilities.* Stillwater, MN: PDP Press, 1992.

Hirsch, Nancy, and Brenda Smith Myles. "The Use of a Pica Box in Reducing Pica Behavior in a Student with Autism." *Focus on Autism and Other Developmental Disabilities* 11/4 (1996).

Hodgdon, Linda A. *Visual Strategies for Improving Communication.* Troy, MI: Quirk Roberts, 1995.

Hypes, Barbara. *Facilitating Development and Sensorimotor Function-Treatment with the Ball.* Stillwater, MN: PDP.

Joe, Barbara E. "Are Weighted Vests Worth Their Weight?" *OT Week* (May 21, 1998).

Johnson, Anne Marie, and Jackie Susnik. *Social Skills Stories: Functional Picture Stories for Readers and Nonreaders K-12.* Solana Beach: Mayer Johnson, 1997.

Kashman, Nancy, et al. "The Use of Videos in Assessment and Intervention of Children with Autism." *OT Practice* July 2000.

Kientz, Mary Alhage, and Winnie Dunn. "A Comparison of the Performance of Children with and without Autism on the Sensory Profile." *American Journal of Occupational Therapy.* 51/7 (1997): 530-537.

King, L.J. "Sensory Integration: An Effective Approach to Therapy and Education." *Autism Research Review International* 5/2 (1991).

Klein, Marsha Dunn and Tracy Delaney. *Feeding and Nutrition for the Child with Special Needs.* Tucson: Therapy Skill Builders, 1994.

Korsten, Jane, et al. *Every Move Counts: Sensory-Based Communication Techniques.* Tucson: Therapy Skill Builders, 1989.

Kranowitz, Carol. *The Out-of-Sync Child.* (Videotape) Las Vegas: Sensory Resources LLC, 2001.

Kranowitz, Carol. *The Out-of-Sync Child.* New York: Berkley, 1998.

Krauss, K. "The Effects of Deep Pressure Touch on Anxiety." *American Journal of Occupational Therapy* 41/8 (1987): 366-73.

Luscre, Deanna M. and David B. Center. "Procedures for Reducing Dental Fear in Children with Autism." *Journal of Autism and Developmental Disorders* 26/5 (1996).

Mora, Janet, and Nancy Kashman. "Strategies for Sensory Integration" *Advance for Speech-Language Pathologists & Audiologists* December 15, 1997 (reprinted: *Advance For Occupational Therapists*; April 27, 1998).

— "Teaming and the Use of Sensory Integration Strategies in Early Intervention" *The Morning News* Spring 1997.

Morris, Suzanne Evans, and Marsha Dunn Klein. *Pre-Feeding Skills.* Tucson: Therapy Skill Builders, 1993.

Motola, Beth. "Using the SI Inventory for Individuals with Developmental Disabilities." *Advance for Occupational Therapists* March 4, 1996.

Oetter, Patricia, Richter et al. *M.O.R.E. Integrating the Mouth with Sensory and Postural Functions.* Stillwater, MN: PDP, 1995.

Parks, Stephanie. *Inside HELP: Hawaii Early Learning Profile.* Palo Alto: Vort, 1992.

Prizant, Barry, et al. *Autism Spectrum Disorders: New Service Delivery Models for Young Non-Verbal Children.* Rockville, MD: American Speech-Language-Hearing Association (self-study publication).

Quill, Kathleen Ann. *Teaching Children With Autism: Strategies to Enhance Communication and Socialization.* New York: Delmar, 1995.

Restall, Gayle, and Joyce Magill-Evans. "Play and Preschool Children with Autism." *The American Journal of Occupational Therapy* Volume 48/2 (1994).

Richman, Linda. *This Is the One I Want.* Solana Beach: Mayer Johnson, 1987.

Sahlin, Laura, and Marilyn Click. *Bridging the Gap: Integration of Therapy and Educational Goals Activities.* Phoenix: EdCorp.

Sheets, Lana, and Mary Wirkus. "Everyone's Classroom." *Closing the Gap* April-May 1997.

Simpson, Richard L, and Brenda Smith Myles. *Educating Children and Youths with Autism: Strategies for Effective Practice.* Austin: Pro-Ed, 1998.

Tanta, K, et al. "Transitioning Young Children to School-Based Services: Perspectives from an Early Intervention Program." *School System Special Interest Quarterly* March 2000.

Trout, Maryann Colby, et al. *SenseAbilities: Understanding Sensory Integration.*. Tucson: Therapy Skill Builders, 1993.

Vig, Susan, and E. Jedrysek. "Autistic Features in Young Children with Significant Cognitive Impairment: Autism or Mental Retardation?" *Journal of Autism and Developmental Disorders* 29/6 (1999).

Wilbarger, Pat, and J.L. Wilbarger. *Sensory Defensiveness in Children Aged 2-12: An Intervention Guide for Parents and Other Caretakers.* Santa Barbara: Avanti Educational Programs.

Williams, Donna. *Nobody Nowhere.* New York: New York: Times, 1992.

— *Autism: An Inside/Outside Approach.* London: Jessica Kingsley, 1996.

Wise, Molly. "Packing Your Simple Technology Survival Kit." *Closing the Gap* February-March 1997.

Wiznitzer, Max. "Why Can't My Child Sleep?: Sleep Disturbances in Autism." *The Morning News* Spring 1997.

Young, Susan. *Movement Is Fun.* Torrance, CA: Sensory Integration International,1988.

Zihni, et al. "The AZ Method: The Use of Video Techniques to Develop Language Skills in Autistic Children." *Autism/Asperger's Digest* Jan.-Feb., 2000.

Organizations and Journals

Autism Society of America, 7910 Woodmont Avenue, Suite 650, Bethesda, MD 20814

Autism Research Institute, 4182 Adams Avenue, San Diego, CA 92116 http://www.autism.com/ari (Bernard Rimland, Ph.D.)

Closing The Gap, PO Box 68, Henderson, MN 56844, Phone: (507) 248-3298 http://www.closingthegap.com (Provides information about computer technology in special education and rehabilitation)

Future Horizons, Inc. 721 W. Abram Street, Arlington, Texas 76013, Phone: (800) 489-0727. Fax (817) 277-2270. Web: http://www.futurehorizons-autism.com (Provides national conferences and books on the autism spectrum; also publishes the *Autism-Asperger's Digest*, a bi-monthly magazine)

Journal of Autism and Developmental Disorders, Plenum Press, 233 Spring Street, New York, NY 10013 (Information about current research in the field of autism)

MAAP Services, Inc., P.O. Box 524, Crown Point, Indiana 46307 (More Advanced Autistic People; Provides a newsletter and other family services)

The Morning News/Carol Gray, Editor, 2140 Bauer Road, Jenison, MI 49428, Phone: (616) 457-8955 (Provides newsletter and opportunities for pen pals for individuals of all ages with autism)

Sensory Integration International, 1402 Cravens Avenue, Torrance, CA 90501 (Provides information on sensory integration research, courses)

Sensory Resources LLC. 2200 E. Patrick Lane, Ste. 3A, Las Vegas, Nevada, Phone: (888) 357-5867. Fax (702) 891-8899. Web: www.SensoryResources.com. (Provides national conferences and publications on sensory integration disorders)

Resources

Autism Program Quality Indicators, University of the State of New York, New York State Department of Education, August 2001. (A self-review and quality improvement guide for schools and programming of students with autism spectrum disorders) http://web.nysed.gov/vesid/sped/autism/apqu.htm

Handwriting Without Tears, Handwriting program by Jan Olsen; 8802 Quiet Stream Court, Potomac, MD 20854, Phone: (301) 983-8409, web site http://www.hwtears.com

Intellitools, Inc, 555 Leveroni Court, Suite 9, Novato, CA 94949, Phone: (800) 899-5587 (Intellikeys, Intellitalk software)

Enabling Devices, 385 Warburton Avenue, Hastings-on-Hudson, NY 10706 (motivational toys, switches) Phone: (800) 832-8697 and Mayer Johnson Company, PO Box 1579, Solana Beach, CA 92075-1579, Phone: (619) 550-0084, Fax: (619) 550-0449 (Boardmaker software)

Therapro, Inc., 224 Arlington Street, Framington, MA 01702-8723, Phone (800) 257-5376, Fax: (888) 860-6254 (oral/sensory equipment)

PDP Products, 14298 N. 59th, Oak Park Heights, MN 55082, (612) 439-0865 (books, oral equipment)

Southpaw Enterprises, Dayton, Ohio, Phone: (800) 228-1698, website: www.southpawenterprises.com (sensory equipment, weighted and "huggy" vests)

Pocket Full of Therapy, Morganville, New Jersey (sensory equipment) Phone: (800) PFOT123, website: www.pfot.com

Ellison Equipment, Lake Forest, CA, (Ellison Press Equipment), Phone: (800) 253-2238, website: www.ellison.com

Special Kids, PO Box 462, Muskego, WI 53150, Phone: (414) 679-3410 (commercial videos for skill development)

Music in the Classroom, Phone:(800) 772-7701, e-mail music@garylamb.com (music 60 beats per minute)

E-mail

Autism Channel Link: http://www.telepath.com\canance\autism.html (internet link to information on autism)

Tammy Glaser: TLGLASER@arctic.net (Parent: source of information for teaching strategies, alternative therapies including nutrition)

Future Horizons Inc. Info@FutureHorizons-Autism.com (books and videos on autism, Asperger's Syndrome, national conferences)

Sensory Resources LLC Info@SensoryResources.com (books, videos, tapes and CDs on sensory integration disorders, national conferences

Nancy Kashman and Janet Mora: janetnancy@aol.com